Between Belief and Delusion

Poetry and Musings

Bruce Nicol

Bruce Nicol was born in Orpington in 1938. Originally from Aberdeen, his family eventually settled in Glasgow. He left school at 15, joined the RAF in 1956, was stationed in Sussex, then Germany and demobilised in 1960. He returned to Germany some months later, initially working in the Berlitz school in Mannheim, then as Flight Safety Officer for the American Army in Heidelberg, where he married Agnes Murray in 1963. He returned to Scotland in 1965 to study Modern Languages at the University of Strathclyde, then taught German andf French in Dumbartonshire before returning to Germany in 1974 to teach in British Forces children's schools and pursue his passion for European languages. He designed a language converter, which anticipated the language apps and instant translators of today, and was regional finaliist in the Toshiba Year of Invention in conjunction with the Design Centre, London 1991, winnning third prize for his language game *lincolingo*. He lives in Hastings, is an enthusiastic local historian amd raises money for local charities with his Old Town Game. He continues to write poetry.

www.brucenicol.eu

With Best Wishes.

Between Belief and Delusion

Poetry and Musings

By

Bruce Nicol

BRUCE NICOL
Sinnock Cottage
Sinnock Square
HASTINGS TN34 3HQ
☎ 01424 431376

Edgerton Publishing Services

Pett, East Sussex

First published in Great Britain in 2019 by
Edgerton Publishing Services
Jasmine Cottage, Elm Lane, Pett, Hastings, East Sussex TN35 4JD
Tel. +44 (0) 1424 813003
Email enquiries@eps-edge.demon.co.uk

Reprinted 2020 with poem 'Undercurrent', page 134 repacing dulicated poem

Copyright © 2019 by Bruce Nicol

Bruce Nicol has asserted his right under the Copyright Designs and Patents Act, 1988 to be identified as the authors of this work.

All rights reserved. No part of this publication may be reproduced, stored in a retrieval system, or transmitted, in any form or by any means, electronic, mechanical, photocopying, recording, or otherwise without written permission.

The book is sold subject to the condition that it shall not by way of trade or otherwise, be lent, resold, hired out, or otherwise circulated without the publisher's prior consent in any form of binding or cover other than that in which it is published and without a similar condition being imposed on the subsequent purchaser.

ISBN: 978-0-9933203-3-0

A CIP catalogue record for this book is available from the British Library.

Typeset in Sabon by Edgerton Publishing Services.

Printed and bound by Ashford Colour Press, Gosport, UK

Dedicated to the Memory of

Agnes Nicol OBE
One-time Director of the
Soldiers', Sailors' & Airmen's Families Association (SSAFA)

The love of my life

"All shall be well, and all manner of thing shall be well"
(Julian of Norwich)

Contents

Development of a Species (continued)

English Language

Farewells

Feelings and Perceptions

Hastings

Human Nature

Contents

Personalities

Relationships

Songs & Anthems

Appendix – Symbolic Meditations

Foreword

Bruce Nicol begins his poem *Alien* by asking 'Am I to leave this place without revealing my strange vision of this world?' While Bruce himself is anything but alien, this book of poems very clearly and often beautifully reveals *his* vision of the world.

And what is this vision? The title gives us a clue. Bruce is certainly no believer in traditional religion or any particular faith and, indeed, he is pitiless in his condemnation of those who try to rule our lives on the basis of either religious belief or political fervour. However, he clearly has a deep belief in humanity. This comes across in so many of the poems, written over 60 years.

It is nevertheless not always clear how much belief Bruce has in himself; he is often self-mocking, particularly in coming to terms with old age, but his humour comes through, not just in those poems that are intended to be humorous (and they succeed), but also often in poems that are deeply serious. It is also interesting that, although many poems are dated, it is almost impossible to put a date on those that are not, the questioning and the thoughtfulness that comes through them remaining unchanged.

And he cares. The poems about friendship are often touching and his love poems, particularly those written since the death of his wife Agnes, are very moving.

The book is divided into sections, but all the poems, except those related to specific events or particular people, are effectively about the meaning of life. One only has to go through the section titles to see this. I could list and analyse these here, but that is unnecessary because readers can do that for themselves.

It is always difficult to decide what is good poetry and what is not. There are many who consider themselves poets, but whose writings are often superficial. That is not true of Bruce. His use of language, often complex and thought-provoking, together with his concern for humanity and for individual feelings and freedom, make these poems worth reading by anyone who shares Bruce's concern for these matters. And the poems in the Appendix, which have been reprinted from his earlier book *Cryptograph*, add an extra dimension to the text in a way that is unusual and possibly unique.

David Penfold

Acknowledgements

My grateful thanks is extended to Dr David Penfold without whose advice and tireless help this publication would not have been possible. Also to Charles Crawford for his patience and wonderful graphics, not to mention my talented daughter, Amanda, who has graciously given her consent to our using her portrait of me on the front cover.

Bruce Nicol

Conflict

The Cabal

O woe and woe and ten times woe
To he who breaks the status quo!
That Man with Evolution has created
Seeking advantage to his condition
As if it were some holy mission
While punishing an unknown foe.

O fie and fie and ten times fie!
On those who raised the Brexit banner high
For they will shortly understand
How long it takes to build a land
And how fast it is destroyed
By a strong but witless hand.

Dread, dread and ten times dread!
False prophets, by ambition only led
By minds unsound, fame and fortune bound
Which care not for the good or ill
Of their fellow men, but only act
To further their own unworthy will.

Shame, shame and ten times shame!
On those who manipulate the lives
Of others like some pastime or amusing game
Who use the ignorance of their prey
With ambiguous words of meaning dark
To shield them from the light of day.

2016

A Short Dash to Hell

Those who think that they should use the violent means
With which they gained advantage without justice
To form a new philosophy are desperately deluded.
For in destroying the freedom of others
They sow the seeds of their own demise.
Like a ship on the rocks in the mighty tempest of revenge
They will be dashed to pieces on the rocks of intolerance
Taking their pornography of bloodshed with them
To the depths and soundlessness of Time.

2016

Breakdown

How is it that you often get annoyed with me
While seldom do I feel the same with thee?
Is it that we tire at last of many years
Together and no longer have the tears
To shed when sadly things go wrong?
Or is it is the fatigue of a life of loving long
The many curious problems overcome,
And petty triumphs sorely won,
That slow erode and sap the vital senses
And rob us of more sensitive defences –
Of differences long concealed
And wounds but recently revealed –
Opinions buried for the sake of peace
Alien perceptions longing for release.
Which happy moments oft dismember
And sad days and weeks remember.
Ah, to forget the stresses without gain
And all the anger and the pain!
For only toleration by both man and wife
Can fain restore the balance of a happy life.

2015

The Traitor Within

Do not bring me your confessions
Nor share with me the secrets of your heart
For I have prostituted that with gave me worth
And lost the noble battle for rebirth
And I must save myself . . .

A vagrant I must tread the ways
Of falsehood and the captive slave's deceit
To gain the baubles of synthetic self-respect
And save my raft which lies already wrecked
Upon a lonely isle . . .

Credit me not with ignorance
Nor absolve me from my fatal fault
Consider not the motives for my defalcating bluff
My false birthright serves me well enough
In the interim . . .

Pity not my circumstance
Nor seek to justify my petty whim
Your human failure is my daily bread
My sickly soul is all but dead
And I must save the rest . . .

Shun my presence if you will
My cunning has already cast the die
For from my influence the weak may never flee
While only strength the beaten mind can free
And such resolve is rare . . .

[cont.

Despise my conscience if you will
My bloody wages fill the moral void
For I am the factotum of your selfish fear
That devil long since my unquestioned peer
Controls my every move . . .

And who am I to comprehend
The intricacies of my master's will?
I would not seek to share responsibility
For those demands upon my loyalty –
Bartered for a price . . .

Nor would I care to give account
For that which penetrates a deafened drum
To stir the dormant soul and snap the brittle heart –
In evil play I but a meagre part
And I feel innocent . . .

Waste not your theory on my fate
Nor grieve the sorrows of insensate times
This only reinforces my corrupt façade
And helps the success of another cheap charade
Of honourable duty . . .

Devouring feasts of double-talk
My belly swells preparing to disgorge
The sland'rous feces of a morbid state of mind
Upon the tables where I lately dined –
Infectious excrement . . .

Flatter me not with sincere words
When I have accusation's blade to hone!
Words are but the opportunist's silvered tools
And honesty's for old men and for fools.
Mistrustful is the flesh . . .

[cont.

Authority is my awful gorget
And equivocation degradation's salve
For I am well-acquainted with rejection's gate
The age of wisdom's reason comes too late
And I cannot return . . .

How can I ever find my rest
When dreamless sleep is but a mystery.
How can I change or ignominious acts atone?
Let me alone, but let me not alone
In case the shot be levied . . .

Trust me not lest I betray
The faith and hope that makes the lazar clean
I fell victim to the lust for easy gain
And I must suffer to the final pain.
I cannot save myself . . .

2005

The King's Shilling

Duty is like a bent and old retainer
Inclined to do the bidding of his master
More out of ageing habit than desire,
And forced by hopeless circumstance
Beyond his paralysed control,
He heeds the glittering fingers
Which beckon him to Fortune's table
To skilfully dispense the juices of excess
And await the thankless pleasure
Of the coronet of social achievement.

It is he who pandering to the whim
Of affluence's harshly jangling bell,
Which governs bonded fruitless task
And with the dogged reflex of obedience
Fulfils the fancies of his lords.
Admitting treachery and fraud
To the extent of household overthrow,
For being by nature servile he will wait
On any master who can pay the wage
Of his unthinking faithfulness.

He tends with dedication strange
The parasitic vines which creep
Across the gardens of the mind
With hidden proliferating strength,
And yet regrets the strangulation
Of more fertile emancipated growths, that
Would feed the hungry longings of the world
Thus sells Man his soul as dust
To become but pale unwitting clay
In the hands of some perverted potter....

1970

Soldier

Gaudy in your uniform
With brasses all agleam
Are you young strutting soldier
Like a member of a team
Of horses, bridled and hitched
To some vast machine
Quite beyond the limits
Of your comprehension.

Daily straining
Within the shafts
Of military dogma,
Unable to escape
The leather thongs
Of a once voluntary domination.

The only hope
Of individuality being
An extra shiny button,
Well-tended coat
Or extraordinary haircut
Accursed signs of little worth
On the bridle-path of government.

Controlled by reins
Held by some unknown master
Far beyond the line of vision.
Blinded by blinkers
Giving access only
To a mass of bland bureaucracy

[*cont.*

The very epitome
Of the military mind
Whose preconceived notions
Of justice must suffice
For all and sundry
With no selection
Or thought given
To the repercussions

Hitherto resulting
From inhuman orders
Expedited by
All too human cogs
Oiled with badges, stripes
And mistaken nationalism.

In troubled times
To fever pitch
Kill Brothers! Kill!
God is on our side!
Victory is ours!
But God does not take sides
In our childish
Petty squabbles,

And such war-cries,
Are ridiculous, meaning only
Kill OUR brothers.
Wherein lies the sense?
Dost thou O soldier
Fail to grasp the implication
Of thy well-armed life?

[cont.

Or does your vacant laugh
Betray a vacant mind?
Is obedience of the body
Servility of the mind?

Dost thou not think
As other men?
Many of your comrades
Have escaped
Only to question or curse
The wasted years

Freedom is not a thing
Of order and conformity
But of love and the protection
Of worldly comforts – false
Those in power exploit
And influence you
With exaggerations, lies
And so-called truths

So that you will
Carry out their plans,
Or is the intoxication
Of the chase enough
To block all fear
And paralyse the mind?
Awake Sir Knight!
Throw off thy armour!
Honesty is hard
But all the sweeter
For the toil!
But alas,
You are duty bound
And rank is cruel . . .   1970

Cold War

That hidden state of gelid strife which lurks
Unseen and with a cunning hardly understood
Way down among the mechanisms of destruction
Housed in unconscious basements of a vile
But necessary self-defence.

That sickly defalcating compromise
Whose safety-valve of futile argument
Functions with an automatic thoughtlessness
Until abnormal activity or intrinsic fault
Engenders total failure and chaotic interim.

A phoney peace of hostile permafrost,
Where meticulously drawn-up arrangements
Do not break forth but hold on to a stalemate,
And having lost all preconceived intention,
Neutralize their counterparts only to be lost

Amongst component hordes of opposing will
A clenched and suppurating fist healed more
By the physician of time than, as some suppose,
The operations of a mercenary order
That can merely mitigate its calculated mode,

But never halt the boiling in its chambers
That propaganda of explosive elements
Derived from the feeble-minded mixing and
Delayed detonation of highly dangerous combustibles,
Controlled by an escapement of nervous supposition,

[*cont.*

Conflict

Hidden deep within the minds of men.
Actuated according to inherent factors
Of unknown intensity and condition,
Constantly subject to the rigours of discomfort
The human conscience struggles on
Viewing strife as a sometime necessary evil . . .

Death

From Beyond the Grave

Spare us a thought
Now we're both gone
Back into the earth of she
Who long since gave us birth
For grieving's is just another stage
Along the edge of non-desired mirth.
Where we are but brief fleeting smiles
In that long sometimes tortured time
That commenced with our beginning.
You ask me why I did not write of you with heart
But I had other things to do than contemplate
The relative delights of our own flesh incarnate
Embodieded in two sweet innocents –
Little girls who gave us reason to exist
So young and shining new
With dreams of many things to do.
While She and I still tried again
To find again that youthful grace
Before the coming sadness that we all must face.
If you feel me quite unjust
Just seek the long past visions
Recorded as we modern humans must
And say that it was just another day
Set amid the annals of an irretrievable consciousness . . .

Lurking in the Shadows

Dark messenger of Nothingness
I see thee not
But know that thou art there.
Wanting to make delivery
Of my reward for chivalry
And a life of striving.
Successful in my failure.

Lurking in the shadows
Thou knowest all but dangers.
Do not betray the time and day
That thou wouldst make the drop
And bring me down expectedly.

2016

Terminus

I know that I am
Past my sell-by date
That soon I must
Confront my fate
Without the help
Of drugs and priests
And other similar
Respected beasts.
I shall have to
Walk alone, to go
To where I was
Before the day
When I was born.
Remember me for
That is all I am.
A memory among
The minds of some.
For others just a
Puff of normal folk
For others just
Another human
Joke . . .

Fretwork

Do not fret for me my dear
Our length of days is not for us to say
Our fates are written far away
Beyond the light of day.
We are but insensate robotic dust
And I will die, as die I must
While you must carry on as you have done
Through the thick and thin of awful years
Despite the pain and incomprehensible fears
You soldiered on with courage and tenacity
Perhaps not always consciously
But always without doubt – heroically.

2016

In Memoriam

The Big Fella's passing by
On his way to that great unknown sky
Which has no colour, scent or light –
Just a warm and painless, endless night
Enfolding all of us when we must pass this way,
On that very private mandatory day . . .

2016

Stardust

In truth it matters not of what I die
'tis the manner of my depart that seems to count
For die I must no matter how it grieves the few
That have become accustomed to my presence
And the banality of this blade of grass.
But think not that I regret my end in any way
For all our ends are written indelibly in the stars
And one way or another we unexpectedly depart
In a natural, lingering, sudden or accidental way.
Weep not for my passing, for it is as natural
As the setting sun after a somewhat tedious day –
More a relief from the final travails of the evening
Before that which was me leaves to become
A part of that incomprehensible puzzle we call life.
No more waiting, hoping or anticipation
No more sadness and disappointment
No more crude ambition or striving for unworthy causes
Nor seeking a more desired slot in the wastes of timelessness
No more anything fulfilling or even vaguely memorable.
No consciousness of anything more
Just another puff of smoke in the eternal sky . . .

For should you see me
In my bier
Weep not
For I'm not here
I am among the stars
The dust of ages, once again
Back at my commencement
A tiny grain
Of the Past . . .

Swansong

Farewell to all that I have known and loved
And hated and despised,
Farewell to life with frenzied passion moved
For death comes in disguise.

Farewell to all that I have seen and heard
And done and left undone,
Farewell to life thou gaudy plummaged bird
Destroyed by mortal gun.

Farewell to all that I have wished and felt
And hoped but never made,
Farewell to gods at whose false feet I knelt
Whose transient blessings fade.

Farewell to all the joy and pain and peace
And restlessness within,
Farewell to sadness – will it never cease?
Will we always sin?

Farewell to soil and water, stone and wood
Sweet luxury of touch!
Farewell to smells like slowly cooking food
When one has hungered much.

Farewell to valleys, mountains, glens and hills,
Highland moors and lochs,
Farewell to heather, trees and daffodils
True dog and cunning fox.

Farewell to music, flippant or with soul,
Worthless or of worth,
Farewell to books – serious or droll,
Sobriety and mirth.   [*cont.*

Farewell to gales and foam-tipped rollers high,
The stirring sting of salt,
Farewell to sun and moon and stars and sky,
The roof of Mankind's vault.

Farewell to truth or falsehood justified,
To well-meant charity,
Farewell to beauty and ugliness defied
And childish vanity.

Farewell to thee mine own beloved part
I whisper in thine ear,
Farewell to thy strange purity, thou quiet, gentle heart,
O would that thou couldst hear!

Farewell to thee and memories of thee,
Sad and wretched some,
Farewell to thy abundant love so free
For now my time has come . . .

2000

Development of a Species

Conception

Amid a twilight sea of elemental broth
And through the eons tossed and turned
By restless storms and undisturbèd calm
Of ages of inanimate disorder,
A certain combination, suspended mutely
On a transient thread of chance
Is fertilized by the mysterious morning light
Of a unique and unaccounted synthesis
And, precipitated into strenuous reproduction,
This fundamental cluster of amazing properties
Is seized with an unearthly urgency,
As though conceived in fear,
Lest its sustaining amniotic tide
Should change and snatch away
The long-awaited gift of life.
Thus is begun a chain-reaction
Of some universal consequence . . .

Growth

. . . and from that tiny speck
Born of errant chemical despumation
And shot through pre-historic seas,
Those precious cells are swept by time
And tide to every global clime in order
To evolve according to the sundry
Characteristics of their new environment
And haply, carried by the currents
Of an aimless restlessness
To re-encounter evermore
Related germs of countless
Differing stages of exchange,
They breed and cross-breed
In an ever-changing hybrid form.

Discursive life, mating in abandon
With unrecognisable siblings,
Or destroying with like energy
Our long-forgotten kin in altercation
Of a cruel and senseless type –
All to win an ill-deservèd continuity
Until the oceans tiring of gestation
And all the fetal kicks
Of its more fractious offspring still unborn
Withdraw unto the deep and form
The sludge of wakeful homicide
To lurk and oftimes die alone
In the diluvium of a foreign world.

[*cont.*

But neuter oceans possess not
The driving force of that dementia
Callèd life, and through a flickering age
Of infinite lunation, those once pathetic
Particles gasping for their evolution
Appear in various forms of change
Upon the land – their fated future fief.

Birth of a Body

But still a nervous war, bearing all
The marks of a primeval urge, is waged
Incessantly among these crawling creatures
Disgorgèd from a briney womb
Into the darkness of inanity,
To evolve teeth to tear the filial flesh,
Limbs to hunt or flee the jaws of
Distant but closely catenated cousins,
And fear, that ever-present fear
Which grows the monster's armoured hide
And builds the rodent's well-concealèd nest!

That all-consuming fear of death
Inherent as the countless cells
On which the corner-stone of life is built.
And so this desultory strife
Drags out between the sighs of time
The seal of basic continuing existence
Becoming indelibly etched on the yellowing
Parchment of animal inheritance
To which a myriad of mutation
Must claim coparcenary – or fall
Victim to a cannibal brutality.

[*cont.*

But one strange creature – quadruped by birth
And long deserted by the fading partners
Of some extraordinary union
Shows promise of an early liberation
From the gelded cage of thoughtlessness.
What occult process makes him stand
In form of hydromanic breed
As though with egotistic pride, a biped?
But even speculation's wild conjectures
Fail to contemplate this bold transition.
A genus doomed to bear the instincts
Of his ancestors as a burden . . .

Primitive Thought

. . . possessing all the facets
Of his ancestral race and all the
Dynamism to depart this ancient order.
Behold he sees visions! and with
Unique dexterity can reproduce
Wild images on walls and roofs of caves.
But with what reason? Decoration? or
Merely to instruct his issue in the chase?
Always that frantic goad of preservation
Creeping disguised throughout the ages!
He resists with evident intelligence
The rigours of climatic chill
And learns to influence the actions
Of his nomad hordes by forced control
And complex systems of communication.
But animal he is, and must abide this state
Until the beast of latent selfishness –
Still starkly undisguised – is slain forever.
That bewildering impediment to progress!
Exemplified by that instinctive battle
With imagined enemies who would stain
The fallow earth of human comprehension
With the scarlet of his unsuspected strength
Until the advent of a burning power
Encourages a still fetal reason
To launch itself into the deceit
Of mastery conceived and born of Man . . .

Dependence

But totally reliant on the favours
Of the one who gave it life,
This helpless, mindless ego,
Clings to the breast of mother's milk
With the desperate thirst of the newborn.
Blind to all but that sepulchral ghost
Which haunts the shadows of the
Undeveloped mind with basic sense
As to what the new event of sight will bring
In the chilly brilliance of awaiting day.
Better a secure tenure of the
Warming womb of senseless peace
Than an undesirèd thrusting-out
Into a world of organised mortality,
Where they must cringe and lie and
Pay lip-service to the powers that be
Who hold the ways to pleasure,
And who would rob them of the privacy
And peace of their new-fangled egotism.
But they are also bound by alien factors
Which prompt them all to seek a ruthless proof
Of their heartless superiority through
Conflict, victory and bondage of the spirit –
That fatal and inherent flaw of character
Whose very birth brings nauseating enervation!

First Awareness

But even the waking awareness of self
Fails to extinguish that destructive fire
Which burns with a persistent greed
In the temples of their simple souls.
Blackening the charitable green
And stunting the growth of progress.

Dense clouds of animal persuasion
Cloak the relativity of selfishness
And intrinsic apprehension of Death,
Permitting only the physician
Access to those occult depths.

The motivation of a lonely psyche
Inherited from a fabian mutation
(To which he must claim descent)
Who trod the pathways of man
Upon his planet in original fear.

He who in the confusion of his newly
Acquired senses and accoutrements
Lacks knowledge of a compleat self
And in this state is unable to coordinate
These novel limbs to his advantage.

Second Awareness

And as a basic thought-process crosses
The borders of another consciousness,
It learns to whip and discipline
These centres of advancèd pattern
Until it can withdraw to cosy isolation
Or project its amaranthine egotism
At will, depending on the circumstances
Of exterior gratification or mortification
For it realises now that it is not alone
And that it holds a burning stick within
Which warms and protects a certain lack
From the ghouls of differing thought that prowl
The wastes of unsatisfactory compromise.

It learns with the instinct of the wild
When to build the gabions of self-defence
Or exploit height to its advantage.
For its subconscious has always been aware
That he who holds the flare is master indeed.

Beginning of Intolerance

But for all the mental acclivity
Of a million years and the discovery
Of many extraneous contrasts
This process of adjustment is robbed
Of the dignity of its metamorphosis
By a darkened urgency which would
Alleviate the crushing burden of its
Reluctantly accepted mortality
By seeking personal well-being
At the expense of its own future.

To come so far and yet to be
Rewarded with such shortsightedness
Is surely the result of over-active
Bellies and underactive minds.
But these dreadful defences, built by
Military mentalities, not castles
Of righteousness are but stockades
Of a deadly, monumental intolerance.

English Language

T – Break

I mourne the passing
Of the central T
For it was really
Meant to be, to
Aid the reader,
Speaker, child
To clear enunciate
Certain words
Whose length does
Render syllables
Difficult to apprehend
Without a guide.
When meaning
Does become obscure,
The absence
Of the phoneme T
In casual speech
Imparts a rather careless hue
To words a common touch
Which English teachers
Do not care for – much.
Sounds like be^er,
Sco^ish, par^y, mee^ing
Ba^le of Bri^'ain
And I would be
An awful milksop
Were I to say
That I would ever miss
The dreadful
Glottal stop!

2015

Gobbledegooook

You have no right
To say that you are good
A statement well misunderstood
For only others have the right
To judge your morals
When all that you are trying to do
Is say that you are well –
Not unwell or ill
But in the best of health
And – unlike the citizens of Alabama
Having trouble with the grammar . . .

2017

Farewells

Goodbye Glehn

Das Englisch-lingo machte Spaß
Wir lernten dabei dies und das,
Wir lernten richtig unterscheiden,
Zwischen all den vielen Zeiten.

Wir lernten all die vielen Verben
"write" und "read" und "die" heißt "STERBEN",
Wir wissen jetzt was "drinking" heißt,
"often" heißt "oft" und "most" heißt "meist".

Wir sagen heut "Did you sleep well?"
Bei lingo lernt man eben schnell,
"This is my friend" so sagen wir,
"We drink beer" heißt "Wir trinken Bier".

Vollendete Vergangenheit
Ich hatte gelesen", Paragraph 2,
"How do you do" heißt "angenehm",
"Go on" heißt einfach "weiter gehen".

"Dear Sirs", so fangen Briefe an,
Wenn man nicht weiß, ob Frau ob Mann,
Für Hirnstein schreiben wir jetzt auch,
Ob er noch einen von uns braucht?

Der "if-Satz", der ganz typisch ist,

Der Hans, ger mal nicht richtig spricht,

Irene "absolute korrekt",

Der Otto mit dem Englisch schockt.

[cont.

Die Gabi hat "a double line",
"ich auch", hört man den Peter schreien,
Die Doris dann noch "lingo" ruft,
"Damn" hört man wie der Bernd dann flucht.

Cornelia ist "up to date"
Christiane auch mal früher geht,
Der Johann ein "good ticket" hat,
Der Bruce mal wieder Witze macht.

Wir waren ein gemischter Haufen,
Trotzdem ist alles gut gelaufen,
Der Bruce hielt uns ganz schön auf Trab,
Die Hauptsach' es hat Spaß gemacht.

Wir haben es uns vorgenommen,
Wir sagen laut "Thanks for coming",
Goodbye, bye, bye and cheerio,
"Frohe Ostern" sowieso.

Anon.

Feelings and Perceptions

Regrets

I now resent the sunny days for which
She longed to somehow ease the pain
Of her protracted and traumatic parting from this place.
How we had planned to visit pastures old and new
And spoken of the happy carefree time
When I was hers and she was mine!
But now alas she's gone and left us
No more her honest, kindly face
Of her sweet self no further trace.
How could she somehow evanesce
Without one final sweet caress
Leaving us abandoned here below?
While she to painless paradise could go,
And by fulfilling her ever-caring rôle
Prepared her precious pristine soul

For its long journey home . . .

2017

Mutatis Mutandis[*]

From the moment
I approached
The world of
Proper men
I felt I was
Supposed by all
The macho pack
To be a mutant.
But he who judges
Modest men
Who unaggressive
Newly met and shy,
The sensitive and fey,
All too often identify
These blameless souls
As gay . . .

Phenomenon
So grand, so strong,
In selfish season,
That it may hit,
Without a reason
To dominate the mild
Of lesser wit
And mind, at any
Minute of the clock
The pack finds fun

[*cont.*]

---

[*] "with the respective differences having been considered"/"Things having been changed that have to be changed"

To bait and mock
Those whom they
Perceive despising free
The sadder lesser
Mortals than they be.
The butt of jokes
For their delight,
But understanding not
What they suppose
Perverse spirits in the fold
Which are just creations,
So they're told,
Of nastiness and
Sick imaginations.

For those too rich
And proud to beg
Ought to be
Brought down a peg
So that they be made
To feel the pain,
Of passing people's
Blind disdain
Of those unfit
To play the game
With better cards.
Thus speaks a world
With little time
For those unblessed
Who find it tedious
To defend their shelf
In a world obsessed
With the unworthy value
Of one's status, sex and Self . . .

Hatred

Hatred is like a diabolical machine,
(Conceived and built of knee-jerk Man)
Which clanks and grates on with that
Dreadful rhythmic din of thoughtless action
Deep in infernal workshops of reaction.

Furnaces roaring with fanatical combustion
Inject their foul envenomed thrust
Into a mess of mental machinery
Maintained by the mindless minions of discontent
Force warpèd wheels and pitted pistons
Into the dizzy clattering revolutions
Of reason hypnotised hypnotised by mythic gain.

Regardless of the shrieking agonies
Of components ruined or worn out
By the grinding of perpetual resentment
This non-productive monster
Hellish in its lumbering motion crashes onward
With spine-chilling inevitability.

Like the old Germanic mills of mass extermination
Foul-smelling in their long-perverted plan
This satanic plant beguiles its workers
And in its irresolute and fiendish cacophony
Drowns out entreaties of humanitarian type.

And slowly the accelerating pace
Of its self-destruction takes its toll –
Overheating cracks the thickest housings –
Intolerable stresses deform components
Long since deprived of mollification.

[*cont.*

In the end a general collapse threatens
As forces of another kind attack
Until the once arrogant and shiny machinery
Of organized persecution falls apart
And succumbs amid the rending, splintering horror
Of the final solution to its own malfunction . . .

1980

Depression

There's not much amiss with you
It's just that rather late in life
The scales have fallen from your eyes
And you have entered an alien place
Over which you seem to have no control.
Thus the fragile bubble of your ego,
Which is your conscious perception
Of your Self, your Life and of the World,
Collides with the fantasy of that significant other
Who seemed to give your existence meaning,
Destroying all the certainties acquired
Throughout the years, and robbing you
Forever of the beloved acquaintance
Who seemed to give you credibility
And sweep away all doubts as to your value
As a member of the human race
But suddenly this awful bereavement!
Engendering feelings of oppression,
Regression and finally paralysing depression
Preventing you from seeing A New Reality
Which is yours, but which must be reclaimed
If you could only 'summon up the blood'
And wrest it back under your control . . .

Mirror

Bland speculum of falsity
Deluding those who come to gaze
With satisfaction or reproof
On shallow, petty human ways!

No crack of imperfection thine
No indiscretion stains thy charm
No ripple sinister disturbs
Thy innocent lacustrine calm.

Defenceless as a child you hang
Suspended by the nail of time
Upon a wall of inane space
Condemned unto a life of mime.

Like some great ashen cliff of kelp
Which dumbly echoes fleeting light
In isometric waves of sham
Beyond the paltry range of sight.

Reflected marquetry of Man
Veneered with sundry attribute
Thy crystalline morality
Reveals its crust of earthy lute!

Beneath a glaze of charity
To those of introspective mien
Who contemplate with bitterness
The foetus of what might have been

Refracted by its own free will
It petrifies between the gloom
Of monstrous truth too dark to see
And fabricated value's tomb.   [*cont.*

But those happy martyred souls
Who view with passion, silvered face
Rebounded flaw and deadly sin
And shadows of a better place,

Await their turn to step behind
That tantalizing limbo plate
Away from all that would conceal
A vision of their mirrored fate.

But deprecate not silent one
Each sanctimonious pseudonym
Which ricochets with deadly aim
According to Creation's whim

From off thy misused countenance –
Ground to reflect and not to damn,
To witness in perplexity
And sadly mimic mortal man.

Consciousness

Who has seen the light
Of Nature's great majestic height
Which towers above Man's intellect
Not considered worthy of respect?
But I alone.

Who can grasp the sense
And consequential recompense
or the convulsions of a life
Fraught throughout with endless senseless strife?
But I alone.

Who conceives a love
A more exalted way to prove
And with a learned humility
Regards all creeds with magnanimity?
But I alone.

Who can find the trust
Amid ambition's wanton lust
To walk unhurried past the door
Of insecurity's enticing whore?
But I alone.

Who perceives the hope
With which he can with joy elope
To find a permanent release
In the embrace of everlasting peace?
But I alone.

[Who is it alone
That can the restless mind atone
And to the faithless offer faith?
But I alone, an unpredicted wraith –
I am Belief.

2002

Alien

Am I to leave this place without revealing
My strange vision of the world
While others do, in terms I which drive me
To the edge of sanity
Because I cannot understand
Their petty point of view?

They seem to me pretentious
And self-consciously poetic
And I do not have the time
To tolerate the sadness
Of their tribal memories.

I am a simple man
With simple expectations, and so
The detailed banality of minds,
Which wish to leave their mark,
And detail all their suffering
Leave me in despair

And swallowing the scream
So belovèd of a voyeuristic press
With time-slots hard to fill . . .
I close my mind to these abominable things,
But feel that I should not.

The pious, mystic dreams
Of those poor devils sinned against
Whose torture I can never hope to apprehend
Bleed me of humanity
And drive me into a hopeless
State of mind.

Filius Nulius

Thou dilacerated offering falsely severed
Thou product of fugacious crapulence
Thou forsaken canvas cruelly despised
Thou foetus of carnelian potential
Thou victim of distempered after-wit
Thou nameless alloy mistakenly conceived
In the melting-pot of human indiscretion.

Who is she who seeks an easy absolution
From the snare of ill-begotten burden
By laying a crib upon the chilly step
Of new flesh deprived of family name?
That red-hot branding-rod of bastards!
That moat in the eye of simpering respectability
Whose crocodile tears befit its patronising smile.

What knowest thou of future tribulation
As thou in unnamed innocence repose
Still with the cream of selfish breast
Upon those tiny living lips? Doomed
To cry the sorrows of a devious path
With naught but ink-stained thought
To guide the falterings of the spirit.

Discarded issue of ephemeral love
Consumed with passion in the flush of youth
But tossed aside when all is given
Like gaudy journals in the evening time
To drift unheeded like rejected flotsam
About the gently heaving surface
Of a fathomless but preoccupied compassion.

[cont.

Thou lonely seed spilled upon the stubble
Of Humanity's well-paved highway of distress
Destined to lament the nipple of good fortune
In some darkened fissure of regret
To wither and die, perhaps alone
Never having overcome that stigma
That sweetmeat of coffee-table gossip – Foundling!

Desertion thou harlot, art thou so insensitive
Or does the stealth of thy post-partum crime betray
The pain'd rejection of a hallowed state?
Pitiful wretch, thy sorrow is but yet to come
For thou in robbing thy own blood of birthright
Hast in doing robbed thyself of more than child
And vindication scribbled in the sweat of conscience
Will never salve the bleeding wounds of thy regret.

1965

Voices

From the unplumbed depths
Of the human psyche
Voices cry to me,
But I am powerless
To comprehend their wailing
For I am just a man
Imperfect in thinking
I am perfect. Yet still
I hear these voices
Often soft, sometimes loud
In a dimension
I cannot understand.

The torture of the soul
Being wrested from the body
Is punishment enough
But this eternal mocking
Drives me onward in despair –
Seeking I know not what
But always dreaming
Of some accessible
Concept for my life.

These haunting voices
Are the insanity of humanity –
The wages of imperfection
But real and endless as the sun.
Warnings, warnings telling me
I am but a moulded pattern
Whose every facet must creep
Into every darkened corner.

[cont.

Have I the will to escape them
Or am I just another face
Of pre-planned obsolescence?
Can I choose, or are my decisions
Rendered sterile by the immensity
Of this vault and drowned out
By the voices from unfathomable
Space that rob me of my sleep
And will to stop the rot?

Things of interest to me
Such as the healing of my mind
Mean nothing to the voices,
For they are not of me
But a destructive view
Of what seems real, but
From which there seems
To be no out without
Enormous sacrifice
Which may well be
Beyond the price
I am prepared to pay . . .

Heidelberg 1963

Reflex

Ye vassals of a monstrous self-deception
In whose fabricated truths and worth
Ye seek the succour of synthetic satisfaction.
Chained to an agglomeration of distortion
We stand, surrounded by the fatuous gewgaws
Of our fancied security – never quite complete
And in this craving state an easy prey
To the grape-shot influence of the unscrupulous
Who would purvey a never-ending succession
Of transcient stimulation for insipid minds
Destroyed by that blinding coruscation of awareness
Found intolerable in its perforating pitch
Suppressed in favour of a tinkling meaninglessness.

Seduced away from the mighty organs of simplicity
By hyperbolic castanets enhanced by false technique
We become the heterogeneous hirelings of a
Multitude of social demigods who control a world
Enveloped in the fetish of political economy –
That vile hidrotic of a universal dipsomania.
We desiccated victims of our own duplicity
Emulating our false idols of power
With the rapturous enthusiasm of Sunday flagellants
Bearing the scourges of shallow atonement
In order to receive advantages
Of an irresponsible and unjustifiable amanuensis –
Hush-money for the fractious conscience
Foliated by the mallet of self-preservation!

[cont.

Frightened into an uneasy acquiescence
By the brutal gantlet of conformity
Whose deified bumbledom brings us to our needs
We tremble at the altar of a chimeratic security –
That tabernacle of fallacious supposition
Which supplies, falsetto, the diffracted psyche
With the relished drippings of depravèd reason
And amulets of financial well-being,
Blazoned forth by the hierarchs of commerce,
Politics and other inauspicious devices.

We are but imbeciles doomed to live forever
In confused awe of that inkling of perfection
Which reoccurs only in the hour of saddened
     contemplation
Following that Gehenna of human frustration
To which we are perpetually goaded
By eternal subjection to a mass of denigrated ideals –
A veritable Gordian-knot of consummate trickery
Wherin the disappointed spirit alternately
Resides in selfish quasi-satisfaction
Or an unfathomed and unreasonable despair
Depending on the condition of its mechanical defences . . .

                                             1980

Hope

Hope is like the glow of coming dawn
Which regularly floods protracted gloom
With the subtle warmth of mystic promise
And in its cyclic beauty
Makes the man of simple vision
Once more the master of his destiny –
For bold is he who holds a candle
Through the void of tragic night
And waits the morn with strength!

So also those who slumber in despair
And early rouse themselves to witness,
Shall forfeit not the comfort of rebirth
Which in defiance of a time of darkness
Breaks forth with an enlightened wonder.
Likewise those who seek release in dreams
And stir the depths of their uneasy sleep
With visions of nightmarish circumstance,
For it is they who toss on restless beds
Or contemplate the night with haunted wakefulness.

They do not reach awareness 'til the midday hour
But finally exhausted go they forth
To bask once more in tardy optimism's ray,
And blinking in contrasting reason's light
Must hasten to perform their many tasks
Before the sunset of a much curtailèd day.
Thus in the urgency of ordered life
The sorrows of the dusk must flee.

[*cont.*

Only those poor helpless souls
Who from accident or birth are blinded
To the spectrum's early morning fire
And with a sightless pessimism
Are doomed to grope their way through time
And in their bitterness to curse
A world of visible dimension and mock
With ill-felt cynicism the saving graces
Or unparalleled delusions of a foolish race,
For they must wait for miracles
Or the pauper's merciful effacement . . .

Poverty

Poverty is like a stick of gum
Chewed with relish by those jaws
That pay the price
And spat with contempt to the dust
When all the flavour has been suckèd out.

Created by the bold relentless turn
Of socialized machines
Which sets the price
And manipulates an inert mass
Into a uniform and passive pack.

Insulated by the silver foil
Of habit's long accepted trend
Which keeps the price
And by its blind prerogative
Monopolizes all integrity.

Wrapped in the tissue of contracted thought
To ward off intuition's germ
Which fights the price
But fails to penetrate the fold
Of fabrication's gay but sterile glaze.

Moulded into any form at will
To justify a fatuous end
Which holds the price
Or in error swallowed down
With other bogus ideology.

Rejected not while in its idle prime
But when its sweetness is consumed.
Who pays the price
Of that production sold so cheap
That it can be dismissed without a thought?

Despair

Despair is like a sick enfeebled mother
A lonely drudge who toils to earn
The drying crust of human faith
Which lies in mourning for a hopeful spouse
Long laid to rest by unmoved sextons
Of the past when time was good
And earns but emptiness in recompense.

She wretched one must heed the hunger cry
Of tragic circumstances scarrèd lung
And empty-handed wait starvation's cot
With tepid water of a pseudo comfort
And pity's poor and dampened fuel,
While products of conception's early joy
Lie dying of privation's painful curse.

It is she who cannot clothe her young
Who whimper in a corner of distress
Beyond the comprehension of her mind
And in their desperate want conceal
Emaciated bodies in a flimsy shawl.
It is she who cannot see the love
Of childhood's glistening trust without a light,
Nor warm the walls of charitable quarters
Without constructive strategy and hope.

[*cont.*

Thus it is she who in her final fall
Into a pit of cruel desolation
Becomes the bloodied victim of a scourge,
That razor edge of Beachy Head,
Some yard's distorted heap of horror,
Or desperate pallid kitchen corpse
For she can only be destroyed
By her own inevitable suicide.

Hastings

A Tribute to Hastings

Known to Vikings, Romans, Normans and the rest
A landing ground before Jesus and Mohammed
And the many medieval English kings were born,
Old England was by the settlement of Hastings bless'd
With its ancient beach-launched fishing fleet
With other ports for the defence of the realm allied,
Threats from foreign ships to meet
And shield us from our enemies upon 'the other side'
Of that great channel which we bold defended
In past times from Spanish, French and Dutch
All of whom from time to time we sore offended
By our kingdom's colonialism and piracy, as such.

Who trod the streets and worked and worshipped
In the ancient churches of what is now our Old Town?
For popular it was in those far-off days when
Britannia under Stuart, Orange and Hanover ruled
Seas and lands a world away from Marine Parade,
Rock-Nore, High Street, All Saints, (with its many
Shops), Winding Street, Tackleway and Bourne.

A frightening, long and uncomfortable journey
In the postcoach from the Swan Inn to London –
Or a still more dangerous voyage down the Thames
And round the coast as did the merchants' ships
Like the Cutter and London Trader that supplied the
Town, albeit known to highwaymen, the Hawkhurst gang
And sundry smugglers, robbers and other desperados
Keen to do the innocent traveller harm or worse . . .

[cont.

Illustrious names, known throughout the civilized world
As the scene of the pivotal Battle of Hastings
Blessed by the Holy Becket
Loved by Logie-Baird
Charmed by Churchill
Adopted by Ashburnham
Despised by Defoe (1722)
Beloved of Belloc, Lamb and Byron
Visited by Victoria and Albert
Excited by Empress Eugenie
Lived in by Louis Napoleon
Frequented by Faraday
Cursed by Crowley
Enjoyed by Eliot and Spencer
Mortified by Morley (1643)
Deceived by Dawson and De Chardin
Reached by a Romanov
Renowned for Ranier and Rosetti
Proud of Potter and her Mice
Grateful to Grey Owl
Watched over by Wellesley-Wellington
And Cloudsley Shovell's mother
Long before the days when Fish and Ships
Became Fish and Chips . . .

2016

Human Nature

Real Men (A Phallusy)

A real man is selfish and cruel and unkind
A bully, a doolie, I think you will find.
They beat women and animals
Drive fast and like mad
Make mothers and fathers
Wish that they'd never had
A creature like that who turned out so bad.

They are rude, they are crude
They gobble their food
They are not very honest,
Nor behave as they should.
It's OK to wreck buildings,
Keep your kids out of school
Neglect obligations and act like a fool.

They treat women badly
Are discourteous, sadly
Because they are witless
They sometimes act madly.
Cowardly pack animals
They take bold advantage
Of physical weakness and feeble old age.

Tatooed and proud
And excessively loud
With vehicles suped-up
This Hell's Angels crowd
Seem unsympathetic
And do what they can, to intimidate
The far less-aggressive, the calm and sedate.

[*cont.*

They don't seem to think,
But excessively drink
Famed for bad manners
They smoke and they stink.
And if they're too noisy
And people complain,
They'll respond violently with language profane.

And they assault young people too
And care naught for the harm that they do
Neither do they admit their guilt
When they their punishments eshew
They rely on uncouth fantasies
With leather, chains and beard
And are by all good citizens afeared.

2016

Mystery Tour

Wound up to twelve
We are let go
Like little clockwork dolls
To jerk and blindly twitch
Along some preordainèd way.

Driven by the obsolete
We tick into an uncertain future
Until our systems start to fail
And the roughness of our way
Begins to take its toll.

Having reached our range
We suddenly keel over
Our tinpot works undone
And so to be ignored –
Of no more interest
Until . . .

. . . at last we are
Picked up
Stood up
Wound up again
And given a new direction . . .

2012

I, Humanity

Objectively immortal, but subjectively mortal
Complete am I
Complete and yet commensurately incomplete.
A perpetual monument to limited perfection
And irrational symbol of love, hate and indifference.
An ocean of emotion and calculation
Sweeping over our requisitioned globe
In never-ending successions of currents cold and warm
Mingling into tepid compromise
Or erupting into a fury of incompatible cross-winds.

A cumbersome beast am I – of prehistoric dimension
Trampling the blooms of innocence into the mire
Of human tradition, dogma and so-called truth.
Licking my genitals in longing for a mate
And eating his tail in animal frustration.
But my dying cells are constantly replaced
By the an uncontrolled will to live another day
And I continue to grow until my very stature
Proves a hazard to everything around me
As I progress through forests of timeless age.

But natural caution must never desert me
For though my monarchy is irrefutable
A certain sustenance I crave – a rare fruit,
Which according to my basic intuition (a belief)
Grows in the highest places of cerebral Man.
And with my proud unbending neck
Wariness is expedient lest my development
Deprives me of this essence of credulity
And unable to prostrate myself, I perish.

[*cont.*

A death of spiritual starvation only to be condemned
To wander on through the primeval forest
By the winding ways of choice
Which, unless exploited by decision
Lead only to a long and desolate nowhere.
A sparrow chirping on the twig of ignorance,
Rejoicing at the warm fulfilment of a summer morn
Questing not a role in life
And careless of the rigours of approaching winter.

A flower, unsexed, of intrinsic beauty
Baring its heart to sympathetic rays
In the morning of life, to whisper dumbly
Neuter joy and vanish in the dusk
A climber, savouring his conquest of the heights,
Full of wonder at the magnitude of Creation,
And humbled by those majestic peaks
Which from my horizon beckon me unceasingly.

An adolescent, rebellious as the youngster
Defying all authority as I must
For this is surely the highest attribute of Man –
The freedom of will and personal judgement.
A babe am I, constantly soiling myself
By mistakes and crying out for comfort,
Wholly dependent on the arms of compassion
And the milk of mother love.

A cockroach, wooing the dung
And infecting all with diseased ideals
Scratching the dirt to find the filth
Only to be destroyed by my own degradation.
A stone, with the symmetry of conformity
Interesting to view, but insensitive and cold
I lie in helpless dejection
Passively awaiting the return of the builder.

1970

Nature of Man

A chaos of conditioning is all
That we in our short lives experience
A confusing mixture of tradition
Scientific fact, belief and raw emotion.

Yet this is our inheritance of madness,
Condoned, nay lauded by those conducting
Bonded lives with little thought as to
The nature of the species to which they must belong.

Unconscious, we record without selection
All delights and mysteries of a known way
With a detail that can finally produce
The integrated or disintegrating personality of Man.

Capable of taking all patterns unto itself
As canvas absorbs the oils of a masterpiece
With each stroke of the master's brush
A portrait emerges layer by layer.

Be the doctrines of our culture sublime or banal
They are a comfort to the simple who seldom
Contemplate the alien standards that they know exist
But take refuge within their own restricted frame.

Still many vegetate within the petty privacy
Of private worlds, but this alone is not despised.
Only when they cannot live within a host society
Without seeking to overthrow its do they become unsafe.

[*cont.*

It is then that they should seek a home among their own
Or return expeditiously from whence they came
And cease to undermine the balance of the status quo
Just because they have failed to come to terms with it.

It is up to Man to avoid the bloodshed of violent change
And not encourage martyrdom for a Belief that would
Lead to revolution, civil war and a generation
Of distress rather than quiet, peaceful evolution . . .

2000

Humour

Alle Meine Enten

Ducks are the greatest comfort
Unto me
For they have taught me
How to be.
To live the life
Of undetermined span
Contentedly.
From intellectual churning
Free.
They quack across the waters
Of the lea
Driving forth my gloom,
Delightfully –
As do their cousins of Peking
With pancakes, hoisin sauce,
And Chinese rice garni.

2015

The Game of Trumps

Mondays at 8 and Fridays at 3 o'clock
The gentlemen appear for their Tarock
At first they're jolly gay and cheerful
But later on they're are not so gleeful.

The first game is scarcely through
When the Professor screams with language blue
"Why don't you play your trump, you prick?
Games like this do make me sick!"

On hearing this the Baron's temper overflows
But rudeness to the others never goes.
Dr. Eberstark undoes the wrong
For his profession makes him strong.

Mr Werner then opens up the door
And calls 'Why don't we play a game for four?"
The Baron, not in a hurry, answers (with a smile)
"Let us three play on a while!"

But the easy-going Mr Werner, is quite adept
The three, now four, have to accept.
And typically they hear his plea
"It's ages since I had a three".

To change his fortune this old crook
At his neighbours' cards he casts a look.
With ire the baron sees this operation
And hides his cards upon his corporation.

[*cont.*

Again a cry rings out to rile
The Baron says "You imbecile"
And Werner clearly threatening says
"Sir, you'd better shut your face!"

Professor Herz can seldom hold his tongue
And often gives his wise opinions lung.
But about such games he's really thick
It's in the cutting – That's the trick.

And those who greedily demand
An early trump
Can scarce control themselves for joy
And sneeringly say "too long here, my boy."

I cannot close this round
By not allowing Kibitz Deutsch to sound.
While playing, Dr Eberstark loved it much
And with respect he spoke of these old gents as such.

The row is over. Love reappears
How can it be otherwise, after all these years?
The following day at 2 o'clock
The gentlemen reassemble for Tarock.

Freely translated from the German 30th October 2011

The Gizzit

As I crossed the Market Square
I saw a gizzit lying there.
I picked it up
And took it home,
For it was my intention
To give it to my wife
For her culinary invention.
But seeing it she gave a scream
And would not let me in.

I cried, "O don't be such a meany
I have to say to thee
I'd really like a gizzit
A gizzit for my tea."

She told me what to do with it
In no uncertain terms.
"Take it to the tip" she said.
"Or feed it to the worms".
("Anyway, I've no asafetida
to cook it!")

The tipmaster would not take it in
And told me on the phone
Because it really wasn't dead
I'd have to dump it on my own.

The butcher said he'd chop it up
And make it into mince
But there was murder in his shop
And no one's seen him since.[*cont.*

[*cont.*

I took it to a carpenter
So he could smooth it out
But he sadly wouldn't touch it
And would only stand and shout.

I tried to sell it, dump it,
Burn it, break it, sell it for a quid
But could not dispose of it
No matter what I did.

I took it to the IRA
To use their gelignite
But when the rotters saw it
They left without fight.

I hoped the dogs would eat it
With poison the doctor did not hinder.
The baker put it in his oven
To roast it to a cinder

The mechanic tried to screw it
To a submarine about to dive
But the damned thing fell off
While it was still alive.

I even asked the Russians
To take it into space
And cut it loose towards the sun
But their President swore
He would not play and risk
A certain loss of face . . .

I took it to the preacher
To hear what God could do
But he said the Lord would not agree
To kill this bugaboo.

[*cont.*

The policeman put it in the jail
To keep it out of sight
But could not keep it in the cell
Without a dreadful fight.

And now I live a lonely life
With my gizzit on an island far away
Still wondering what to do with it
For ever and a day . . .

2016
(*With apologies to Danny Kaye*)

Goddess

Godis, Goddess! healer of my soul
While trying to keep by body whole,
With potions costing more or less
By courtesy of the NHS,
And despite the ravages of Time
She tolerates my geriatric line
Of ancient jokes and idiotic quips
Like the face that launched a thousand ships
Calm and peaceful, understanding she
Just as a sympathetic medico should be;
An expert in the human humours
And mindful of the bleakest rumours
Regarding antibiotics – and cynical titters
About the power of Swedish Bitters
And other homeopathic remedies
That kept me fit throughout the years
Assuaging all my ageing fears
Of decrepitude, disordered mind,
Disease and other horrors of that kind
Deafness, blindness, incontinence
And horrid things that don't make sense.
For what could be worse,
Before you're in the hearse
Than dementia when you can't tell by far
Who, what or where the bloody hell you are.
Without a doctor such as she,
Who does not judge but cares and smiles
While seeing me through my final crumbling miles
Helping me bear anxiety and pain
Treating me well, 'til I come back again . . .

Christmas Greeting

Before we all expire with gloom,
Or kill the messengers of doom,
Let us rejoice for these few days
And contemplate the peaceful ways
Of One who did not mind some drinks
And celebration feasts, methinks;
Who understood divinity
And the sin of inequality.

Forget the mortgage and the rent!
This season is by Heaven sent . . .
Forget the job, the crime and strife
And Eurothreats to British life . . .
Remember to give the needy reason
To bless your thoughtfulness this season.

1980

The Corbie

Hoots, mon, have ye heard?
The Corbie's here, a weird auld bird,
Carnaptious and an ageing rebel
But loved by many, I've heard tell
Although he seems to lack the beak
That certain of his cohorts seek,
His daily cycle taks him doon the toon
Where he perches like some auld tuchun.
Sae principled he canna tak a stand
Tae see the raptors aff his land
And when the awfu' shadows fa'
He'll not defend his flock at a'!
At best he'll try some intellectual mobbing
With quillèd hoi polloi hob-knobbing.
His left wing does not understand the right
He'll more confuse his followers than fight
An intellectual, he's more inclined to squawk
Than dally with his enemy, the great blue hawk.
Squeamish, he will caw and carp defensively,
Atop his idealistic tree.
And when danger comes, he'll bitterly complain,
Rightish flights of fancy loud disdain.
Sycophants flock where he can dae nae wrang
Where this endangered species,
Murmurs its pacific sang.

And when sad decisions must be made,
He'll soon forget his principled crusade.
Behind his idealistic rationale he'll hide
And by his mother's nest he'll bide.
He micht hae been a predatory bird
But that would be quite, quite absurd . . .   2015

Incisor

I bless that happy afternoon –
When apprehensively
I stumbled up the stairs
For complicated dentistry repairs
At the magic hands of Wizard Poon . . .

I need not have worried, for
His skills are peerless,
His patience long,
His point of entry –
Old Hong Kong . . .

2015

A Ballad

One day a general of great fame,
To Heidelberg in county Baden came.
On mighty steed this knight did ride,
With full company and aide beside.
And as this train the fortress grim approached,
The aide the subject of promotion broached.
"Faith Sire," cried he with eyes of tears.
"I've been a captain now these twenty years!"
"And shall remain so, wretched churl,
So long you act as virgin girl
And nothing of importance do report."
Was the great soldier's tart retort.
This caused the aide to cogitate,
And as they did the courtyard penetrate
A stranger he espied – with unaccustomed air
And – gadzooks! – the very minimum of hair.
Indeed, so short it did appear
The man was shorn from ear to ear.
Hairless yea on lip and chin!
Which seemed to aide a shocking sin
That one should cut off what the Lord
Had given him – with sharpened sword!
"A dreadful, ghastly deed," quoth he,
"And not the least bit milit'ry."
So diligent did he inquire
The nature of this peasant's hire.
A knight called Petit standing near
Perchance this inquiry did hear
And answering with concealèd smile
Replied for all the rank and file,

[cont.

"Why that's the bard of Aberdeen,
In taverns and bordellos never seen.
A Scotsman virtuous, philosopher and poet
(Though to see him you'd never know it).
Although he stands in rags and tatters,
He is an expert in all Army matters."
"By my beard and whiskers," swore the aide,
He improves what God himself has made."
And to his everlasting shame,
He took the foreign fellow's name
And to Commanding General went
(Seeking promotion was his bent)
"Great King," quoth he, "a good idea have I
The problem of differing faces to defy
And to control our quaintish rabble
Foul with lechery and treach'rous babble
Conducive is; and through its uniformity
More pleasing is unto your cultured eye.
I propose that every man his whiskers trim –
Indeed, if I might venture – to the skin –
If it do please your Highness."
Thou damned and poisonous serpent,
Wallowing with pleasure in the excrement
Of thy own evil fancies. How dare thou!
This impertinence thou will surely rue;
To rob men of their personality
An insult is unto the very Deity.
Of wretched egotism yours I tire
Henceforth be just known as common squire."
Thus spake the wise and much revered king.

[*cont.*

And then the aide he did a dirty thing –
Straight'way went he to the man
Who all the trouble had began
And smote him on the cheek a smarting blow,
And said, "I think that you should know
That you, by Gad, a beard must quickly grow
Or to the Devil of the North had better go –
Thy face nevermore in Heidelberg to show."
Then answered the Bard with intonation low,
"So shall it be," and clear inflected,
"I shall return where individuality's respected
To Scotland, where all men are free
And balmy breezes blow in from the sea
Pleasing to the nostrils – and the River Dee,
Whose banks so oft my pillow were
And where good men do rightly so deter
Non-constructive criticism – so
Before I strike you down, thou had better go
Back to your master, which he did –
A wiser and more humble man who,
For selfish motive had the gall
To criticise, (which was not his due)
And in so doing it, lost all.
Pay heed all ye that out of turn do speak,
For thou art just another man – and weak.

Poissons d'Avril

The salmon and the sturgeon
Went swimming out one day
And thought it might be fun
To hatch a plot, they say,
To free themselves from foreign kind
And have the little fish believe
That it was just a wheeze
To gratify the shoal's primeval dream
Of power, and tweak the snouts
Of godless enemies downstream.
Unlike them and with no sole.
Their argument did not reveal the pain
Of abandoning safe waters
For the possibility of gain.

Soon they braved the waves
And storms of hustings chance,
Heedless of risk and free of conscience too
They confident of success did ask
The other fish a course to sue
For independence from the English shore
Which many felt to be untrue.

Alas! Alec! Things went not well upon that day
For too many denied the deuce
Their vote to have revenge
For ills imagined or abstruse.
That day both misjudged the mood
And lost the vote as well they should.
Beware disloyal whelk and sprat
And other so-called friends like that . . .

On Calverley Hill

I like your modus Doctor Poon,
I'd gladly lie from dawn 'til noon
Upon your magic dental chair
Within your prostodontic lair.
Assisted by the lovely Jane,
Judicious jabs of Novocaine
And kindly words, you do your part
While music calms the nervous heart
I'm grateful for your skill, good Doctor Poon
So I'll be coming back in June . . .

Written with gratitude while receiving painless and highly
efficient bridgework 15th May 2012

Judgement and Opinion

The Wasters

Woe to those who while away their precious lives
With scandal, gossip and excessive entertainment
And the inexcusable idleness of grumbling!

Those who would allow the precious sand of mortal span
To slip through their unconscious fingers
To be lost forever in the swirling desert dusts of Time!

These are the wasters, blind to the glass of fleeting years
And the vision of their personal expiration who play
Boredom's games and curse the industry of others!

What has meaning in the minds of those preoccupied
With triviality and feelings of their own importance?
The lives of the famous and all the social humbug of success!

The rewards of speculation, casual encounters of a carnal kind
And over-indulgence render real achievement hollow
Thus falsehood becomes a currency to be admired.

Oblivious they squander their potential in pursuits
That rot the mind or in distress do seek forgetfulness
In transient pleasure and restless intoxicated slumber.

Those slaves of Mammon soon awake to find
Their productive time is gone and they are left
With nothing but the poverty of riches in old age.

They only have the ear of Death to listen to their
Plaintive calls and promises to lead a better life.
Alas it is too late and silent is the grave of foolishness.

But Wisdom has a different life to lead
For it is always conscious of the wonders all around
And nourishes all the corners of the soul.   1970

Morality

Morality is like a candle flame
Which burns unseen within the mind of Man
And lights the pointless shadows of the way
With forms of tangible advantage.
Constant in its being, but whimsical
In intensity it flares or flickers
According to the pressure of the social draught.
Thus in the tranquillity of principle fulfilled
It is a beacon which with steady brilliance
Floods the path of those who seek direction.
But in the breeze of change it wavers,
Casting shadows that beguile
The vascillating footsteps of the fickle.
And when the winds of Man's ambition blow
To stir insidious currents of dishonesty
His torch becomes a spluttering symbol of virtue
Shedding its random rays in vain
Upon small aspects of his route
And robbing all his senses of perspective.
And when by swirling gales of revolution
The flame is lessened to a feeble glow
Its bearer is abandoned to the darkness
Of a baser motivation to blunder onwards
Through the fright'ning wastes of human recklessness.
There this brand of personal enlightenment
Should be maintained at any cost
To burn with maximum intensity
Throughout the rigours of the night.
Serenity and strength must shield
Its delicate combustion from elements
That would impair a sacred trust
Lest the way be lost and not regained . . .

Honesty

Honesty is like a towering pillar
In the temple of a personal morality
It is a column of truth and purity
Which lifts its noble form on high
In monumental defiance of those latent evils
Which would with perverted rejoicing raze
Its regal splendour in rubble to the ground.

An emblem of fidelity, it reaches
Upwards from the nave of basic reason
Into the very dome of Universal Sense,
And by its inveterate construction becomes
An architectural isthmus bridging
The void between our earthly folly
And the highest aspirations of Man.

Raised not by fickle chance nor by
The purse of that imperious command
Which lauds the worship of fallacious gods
And seeks with ostentatious piety
To curb the firey tongues of devastating conscience,
But by the scarred and boney fingers
Of awareness which hide its dumb expression
In the meditating chasms of enquiring minds.

[cont.

This is the craftsman, who with modesty and skill
Fashioned every stone with ethical precision
To harmonize with all the factors of his will
For his experience of disastrous structure
Fills him with the patience of the artist.
He therefore builds, not for petty payment's
Transient intoxication but for the subtler joy
Of contribution to and anticipation of
A foreseeable entity of ultimate perfection,
Erected proudly and with love according to
The absolutes of intellectual judgement.

Thus was the granite of unyielding character
Melded with old resolution's mortared trowel
To accomplish a sublime and holy union
Reinforced in order to withstand the shocks
Of corrupt or shaky grounds, it glitters
In its morning majesty and though the sun finds flaws
Within the crystalline material of its face
The shadows of the evening light reveal
The richness of its pattern . . .

1980

The Anointed

No matter what you call your God, He or She occupies the same stage in time and space. All we know is that we are all brothers and sisters and therefore no one is exalted above the rest.

There is no welcoming committee or feasts in those corridors – only the familial joy over the newborn as they grow, and the mourning of those we leave behind. Status does not guarantee or even justify access to the fabled world of someone else's dream.

This may be of little comfort to the many, and outrageous blasphemy to those with fixed beliefs, but sadly all we really have at a physical level, is the comfort of food, drink, shelter and the companionship of others while we live.

Mentally, we have our imagination, the concept of danger, the awful vulnerability of neglected children and their misguided parents, and what will become of us all.

May their Gods help the pious who have to live and love without the notion of eternally rewarded lives in a heaven elsewhere counterbalanced by the belief that we are superior and will one day benefit from our primitive, insensate lives of blinkered self-delight, instead of freedom, fairness and a sense of fraternity.

Power is the problem – for it corrodes the mind, and hoodwinks the intellectual lightweight into believing nonsense which can seem rational and true, but which can in the longer term wreak havoc in the affairs of men, and bring disaster on us all.

[cont.

Terrorists taste a little transitory power over their fellow humans because they have been told that they are God's anointed and will be rewarded for their belief in a bogus hereafter invented by a blameless elite who knew no better than we do now, but who are by no means averse to using holy books to service and consolidate their power.

In order to subjugate the naïve and innocent and have them join the ranks of zealots who one day will perpetrate the most atrocious crimes in the name of their god, they promote a creed which seems to hate its fellow men and hold them culpable for what their holy men have designated sinful.

But what do these petty preachers know? – only the texts of their holy writings and the rules, lessons and traditions which their kind believe should be propagated for the good of Mankind. They are not bad men – only victims of their powerful belief systems . . .

Tonsorial Observation

What is it about a tuft of facial hair
A badge of faith for some
That gives unthinking men the right
To behave like God's own son?

How is it that a belief like that
Allows the undeserving male
The rights of others to impale
And feelings of superiority begat?

What kind of mind incites the innocent to kill
At random strangers who bear him no ill
And teaches service to his God with violence and bile
And medieval executions vile?

Submitting to a God he will not share
His inappropriate garb he cherishes
To worship what may not be there
While half the world in fear perishes.

He believes his ancient, peaceful creed
But has corrupted it according to his need
That others also obey unthinking as he prays
And dreams about the end of days

When he will ascend to luxury and licenciousness
Denied to him upon this Earth
Which, while alien, gave him birth
Supplies the answer to the need
And absolutely no ideas of his own
He submits to a God he will not share

And domination
With other members of the human race?
What monumental fear causes them
(No matter what he calls him)

Real Beauty

Beauty is a seagull on the wing
The promise of a diamond ring
A pansy smiling in the sun
A game of cricket fairly won
Creations of great brush and pen
The glory of the moor and glen.
Willow's shade and tumbling water
Devotion of a son or daughter.
The striving of disabled youth
The comfort of unvarnished truth
The miracles that work achieves
The drugs that agony relieves
We understand when we are older
That beauty's only in the eye
Of the sensitive beholder . . .

Love

Leaving You

(But oh my dear)
I must leave you now
And sail away
Unwillingly
And sad perhaps
But that is the way
Of things we feel
Within this place
Where we are doomed
To love and finally
To die.
I shall always
Think of you
No matter where I
Am and how
I feel

2016

Tribute to a Special Person

Oh Sister Agnes, laid so low!
Full of courage on you'll go
Making life better somewhere new,
Where you will nurse beyond taboo,
Putting yourself behind the host
Of those who love themselves the most . . .

2017

55 Years On

Many years have passed away
Since that amazing happy day
Which neither of us can forget
When first by happy chance we met.

You steal my tales
You tell me what to do.
But I don't mind
Nor our relation rue.

You like to be in charge
But neither knit or sew
You tell me what is going on
And show you're "in the know".

You do not drive
Nor ever wash a dish
You are the Reading Woman
Who cooks me what I wish

And now despite this awful rhyme
Not meant to wound or hurt
Will you still be my Valentine
Misunderstandings to avert?

2016

Homecoming

I am coming home, my dear
For without you, I cannot rest.
I am only half a man, a lost soul
Seeking your blessed direction
And the peace you bring.
It has been so wretched long, –
Too long for loving hearts like ours –
To be upon this rack of sadness.
The pain of this state of melancholy
Is only bearable when I recall
The last time we were together,
Or anticipate our next embrace . . .

2014

Coronation

One day a stranger with a golden crown
Arrived in ancient Hastings town.
Right regal, he did bring the shining light
To spread around and make things bright
Through the magic of electric power, he sought
To gain from local peasantry support.
He brought his bride the Princess Rachel,
A peaceful, green and modest angel
To comfort him in later years
And rid him of a single man's pathetic fears.
And that's not all. Like an Indian potentate
In the Imperial Raj of late
He's marrying her in the Durbar Hall
Carved for the Crystal Palace show of 1851
For the railway magnate, not to be outdone,
Moved to Lord Brassey's Park Lane home
And from there hence
To his new Hastings residence
Sandalwood, cedarwood and sweet white wine
For a wedding such as this sublime.
King Graeme and Queen Rachel fair
We wish long lives devoid of care!

Essence

Your essence is a vision only I can see
In fleeting moments – always unexpectedly.
For I could not compare thee to a summer's day
Or to a rose whose scent and beauty fade away –
Rather some phenomenon of psychic space
Whose powers all petty ponderings displace.

You skim unfettered by objective time's constraint
And egotism's smug but aging taint
Across the margins of that inward lake
Stirring its waters gently in your wake.
Unpredictably you spin and weave
Flaunting the laws by which men live.

And though you know the secret ways
And all my hidden senses tantalize
We always fly together you and I
Through the darkness of that inner sky.
Speed and attitude we wakeful trim
To match each other's instinct, need or whim.

And though I follow you upon your errant flight
In and through and of insensate night
You still beguile, surprise, confuse
And fill the vacant moments of my muse
With joy, anticipation, sadness
Insecurity, despair and even madness.

[cont.

Love

For you are part of other dreams and places
One face I know, but there are many faces . . .
Bathed in new light as alien suns draw near –
Blazing like dawn across the Stygian air –
You sweep aside the gloom and come to me
Thwarting my wanting will – capriciously.

But when the silent shadows fall again
And ambiguity once more controls your train
I could not cheated change my congruent course
For I am held beside you by an occult force
Which some call Love . . .

1980

Dance

I look at you again
And see not what my eyes have seen
But what my unknown self
Has partnered in some erstwhile dream
Which curiously lingers on within me
Not as a memory
But as a mutant portion of my substance.
As compatible essences mingle
In exquisite flux,
That which was and is the truth of us
Still pirouettes – but more sedately now –
Beyond the limits of unconscious error
While our appearances, acquisitions
Stumble on bemused, seeing only that
Which youthful eyes are wont to see.
I dare not contemplate a rhythm so innate
Lest harmony desist or I forget
That measure which I seem to know
Yet know I never learned.

© Bruce Nicol 1980

Love

Love is like a mountain spring which bursts forth from the
    bondage of an
Overflowing heart to spill in splashy splendour on its
    downward path
To the parched plains below. Tumbling in twinkling torrents this
Cascading crystal's clarity deceives the imperceptive eye
And what would try to block this flow contrives its own
    eradication.
The rough is reamed and rounded in the gentleness of its caress
And finally the most stubborn resistance succumbs to its
    insistence.
Some dwell in close proximity to this refreshing stream, but
    other hearts
Less fortunate, are born to live apart and only quench their thirst
In less-palatable waters, which twist the timbers of their spiritual
    homes.
But clean cool currents, filtered fresh by strata old as time itself,
Generously free by Nature given, not recycled nor transmogrified
Into something tasty to be be hawked around for cash,
But the pure and simple elixir that slakes the thirsting of
    the soul . . .

2012

How Do I Love Thee?

I love thee as the shepherd loves his own
Upon the moors of chilly human trust
Waiting the dawn apart, but not alone
I crouch in your affection's warming dust
And conquer boredom's apathetic sleep.
Stray not from me but stay a lifetime near
For I am Man and Man his love must keep.

I love thee as a father old and proud
Of Life in passion's wanton moment sired
When he to differing mode of Love avowed,
By heights of optimistic Youth inspired,
Was moved to plant the seeds of Parenthood
And thence in apprehension wait the day
When his new bloom maturing blows away
Upon the the breeze of cyclic Nature's Mood.

I love thee as a bold and selfish youth
Secure in false propriety pride
Whose baubles blind the searching eye of Truth
And passing shadows of possession hide,
For hapless he will rue the day of Sight
When Earthly goods take on their transient shape
And from the gloom of ignorance's drape
Appear in stark appraisal's Light.

[*cont.*

I love thee as I love my far-off land
Not with foolish misdirected whim
Nor shallow homesick Patriotism bland –
Rather deep longing undefined but for the while
Sweet perfume of unpolluted air
And firm resolve of unexploited Earth
Whose unpretension gives me thoughts of worth
And guides me from base Motivation's lair.

Heidelberg 1964

Immature Love

It is as now that I recall
The bloom of that forgotten love
Which we so passionately did share
A love that asked no questions
Made no demands.

The evenings – blessed earthy time
When I was yours and you were mine
How is it that such things can change?
That love can ebb and flow
As ocean tide.

The mornings – how can I forget
The sleepy smile, the murmured word
That shook my very being through and through?
A smile of well-adjusted youth
In this infernal world.

How often did we see the light?
Knowing our earthly sins full well
But finding solace in eachother's arms.
Victims of cruel destiny
And a Godless age.

Victims we were, but happy ones it seemed
Trying at times to shut the darkness out
But mostly caring little what the future brought
Completely dominated by the spell
Of a strange compulsion.

[cont.

"We were mad," cries out my tortured soul
And yet how is it possible, I say,
To discount this delightful time as sin?
God in Heaven, hear us now
And try to comprehend!

It seems so long since we were naturally wed
And memory such a wretched temperamental thing
Which only chooses to reflect
On tragic happenings of the Past –
The sensual to forget.

O conscience still in evidence
How is it that we suffer yet
The grumblings of a disappointed spirit
Which we alone must bravely bear
With vacillating minds.

We were too human you and I
And all our concepts foolish, immature
But we parted – all too soon
Ere our imperfect love became
The prey of insincerity.

The parted lips, the outstretched arms
The scented body waiting to be mine
The long embraces mingling with symphonic beauty
The whispered nothings, passionate and warm
All but fantasy . . .

1967

Sonnet 1 for Agnes

As our chances of survival whole decrease
We should not let our joie de vivre die,
And all criticism of one another now decease
For such transactions foul the memory
And perceptions of our foolishness disguise
While crackling fires sad old resentments fuel
Freeing unworthy thoughts, and even lies,
Destructive fettered inclinations cruel.
The weakness in ourselves to circumvent
While keeping closed that dang'rous coilèd spring
Of thwarted egos rendered malcontent
By exhortations to consume unceasing
Thus find the injured in your loving care
To bless the day your duty helped them there.

2016

Valentine 1

When there is nothing left to say
And we are grateful for another day
I think of us as once we were –
Young and beautiful but knowing little –
With likes and dislikes irrational and fickle
Work, ambition – personal needs
Only now the Past's potential seeds
Which perished after having grown and bloomed,
By years and failing faculties consumed
We still dance our dance, but slower now
Our steps less sure in time contracted
We see each other in an ev'ning light
Governed by habit, familiarity and age,
We waltz along some quiet predestinèd way
To music chosen by our tempered love.
Still critical, but only hoping to improve
We care not for the time of day . . .

Valentine 2

We strive to maintain fantasies –
But no matter.
We fight to retain identities –
To no avail.
We struggle to defend our rights –
But we have none.

For we who give voice together
Rejoice together
Are as one.

We who stay together
Stray together
Beyond the pale –
Believing our small speck a landmark
Ourselves do flatter.

But we who hope together
Mope together
Toil together
Spoil together
Rest together
Are best together.

For though we on occasions
Hound each other
Confound each other
Hate and bait
Confuse, amuse
Curse or nurse each other –

[*cont.*

We two who turn together,
Learn together
Delude ourselves
When it may seem
We could alone
Survive this dream
Apart

For in love we live . . .

Modern Living

The Birth of Clockwork Man

Featureless faces
Whose blank expressions
I shall never see
Clinical hands
Whose detached fingers
I shall never feel.
Numbered voices
Whose congruent accents
I shall never hear.
Drowned by the roar
Of rationalisation
Lost in a maze
Of mass production
And like the soldiers of war
Replaced as they drop
In their anonymity
Only to be once more
Swallowed by a mess
Of machinery,
And swept away
Into the obscurity
Of oblivious repetition
Of learned reflexes
And automatic tasks.
All in the name of the Economy!

[cont.

The God of malnutritioned Man!
No more the ruddy smile
Of farmers at the door
Selling the products
Of their sweat
With country jests
And sincere mien.
The scarred and gnarlèd
Fist of unmanicured
Simplicity and
Personality unvarnished.
Rich in the brogue
Of the pasturelands
And simple knowledge
Of the soil from which
He with equal skill
Has coaxed the favours
Of his chequered livelihood.
While his counterpart
Of nowadays must fill
The quotes and contracts
Of the real money-makers
With the mechanised madness
Of regulated clockwork.
All in the name of progress!
The opiate of malnutritioned souls.

1970

Mobile Phone – Smart Alec

I'm never alone, with my mobile phone
It affords me company
When I am far from home.
It will tell me what I owe
How far and where I have to go.

Of sin and crime and sex and birth
Its facts give my opinions worth,
All human knowledge at my hand
Empowers me, making me a king
Feeling confident of anything.

My smart companion never fails
To keep me up to date
It helps me never to be late
For it's a diary, calendar and clock
Music library, from classical to rock.

It may de-skill me, help me
Rob me of my wits
Deprive me of Life's interesting bits
By providing certainty where there is none
And computer-generated fun . . .

But where on Earth now would I be
Without this new reality?
I'd be lost for ever – like some tiny ship
In a howling gale's distress
Endangered without its GPS.

[*cont.*

A smart device, but lacking soul
Which sometimes seems to make us whole
But having no kindly element
It is just like money – cold and loveless –
Just another thing for rent . . .

Refrain
Let me give you good advice
Always take your small device
When into the big, bad world you go
My smart companion tells me so.

2016

Musings

Mistrustfulness

People cannot be trusted
For they alter what you say
Before they pass it on
To spend another day
Spreading unwise gossip
And the mongering of rumour.
They mis-hear, mis-take
Mis-understand, and mis-report
Almost everything they hear
For there's many a slip
Twixt ear and lip
As the proverb rightly says.
For accuracy and the truth
Do not seem to feature
Among such interminable natter
Of those so sure they apprehend
What you are likely to have said
According to their template
Of some person just like you
Where the truth and all that
That entails, does not seem to matter . . .

Cryptograph

Father you have passed
Your message on to me
And know its content not,
Whatever it may be.

But deep within –
Beyond the petty grasp
Of individual whim
Its ciphers mystically rest

Til clasped unto another's breast
I witless pass its precious substance on,
To aid or mellow or destroy
A formless father in Eternity.

2015

Concept

What is this conceived in joy
And brought forth in contracting pain
To live a life of undetermined span
And in death return from whence it came?
The merest concept of a plan
Born of the urgent soul of Man
Is that which comes in infant form
Unique in its potential height
But fearful of the powers of change
And therefore anxious to assert its right
Before its ideals lose their range
And are annulled by conflicts strange.
Maturing subject to the drum
Of legions of conformity
Which call to arms the pithy seeds
Of Fear's demented insecurity.
Thus amid psychotic weeds
Deprived of more important needs
An idea tends to putrify
Unless by chance new strength is found
Through marriage with a differing strain
Of that same thought, but in more fruitful ground
There in sympathy to gain
And find at last its true domain.
So fairs a theory unto death
To live to learn and learn to live
And from contrasting practices to glean
But always of itself to gladly give
To those who would improve their mien
Or failing, on its wisdom lean,

[cont.

Until disproved or superseded
By the offspring of its thought
It is with honour laid to rest
By grateful students it has taught.
Having stood the acid test
It leaves but Memory's bequest . . .

1995

Crux

Who is he who hangs about a Delphic
Pillar of corrupted good, bearing
The bloody spike of human triviality
In patience or despair?

Who sheds the tear of unadulterated pity
At the inveterate malady of Mankind's
Irresolution, and slakes his dying thirst
Upon the bitter sponge of artificial progress?

Who wears the thorny crown of unabated
Torment with dignity, while from strange
Vantage views the vast necropolis
Of a seldom exhumed awareness?

Who in frustration views the sinking
Quagmire of a charnal-house
Of obese satisfaction, enacting
Passion plays with sanctimonious myopia?

Who must endure the pious chanting
Of an imbruted people people stagnating
In malpracticed rependance amid the
Fetid pools of interpolated lithurgy?

Who listens with silent understanding
To those of simple mien who offer
Sincere and unpretentious loyalty
To an impaled but undying God?

Know they or care who strut through life
With alvine pride and spurious motivation?
Those haberdashers of obdurate pardon
Selling their souls for a mess of the Proverbial pottage . . .

[cont.

Petty psalmists of a popish prerogative
Scratching coronachs to the dead who live,
Well-meaning murderers who kill not in the
Smutted name of revenge, but in the
Impassioned name of Justice . . .

The so-called benefactors of the race
Filling the atmosphere with the noxious fumes
Of discontent among the alleged misfortunates
Attacking Death where Life has little meaning
And creating dependency through promises
Of betterment . . .

Those despotic hierarchs of religious orders
Extolling the Decalogue only when it seems
Politically expedient to tolerate morality,
But when killing must be done,
Bolstering the Confused and ductile
With fallacious reasoning
And impossible justification . . .

In peace the fulsome opiate of the insecure
Meting out the vivifying Eucharist to those
Frightened by their own self-made mortality –
Sacrament-mongers peddling their wares
To the faithful who seek the ambrosia of some
Elesian bower and ill-deserved alleviation
From the unfaced dilemmas of Life . . .

Pragmatical burocrats in their celibate cassocks
Who with degrees and encyclicals influence
A mass of warring factions to unite in faith
But forget with their deluded sense of mission
That dogmatic enthralment is the rectory
Of false homage and rebellious pasquinade
And a refuge for internecine insincerity . . .

[*cont.*

Those petty pontiffs, filling the weak-minded
With homilies and tedious legends,
Pious warnings and firey sermons –
The popular purveyors of excuse who
Preach the fulfilment of their desirata
And teach the flunkeyism of engendered
Bigotry in a coagulated Christendom . . .

Complimenting all the breast beaters
And pseudo-carriers of the cloth, the plebeians
Unsure of their perfection, gladly shed
Their tears of Sunday atonement and hope
To win a heavenly reward by wooing priests with sweet
Sherry and brown Windsor soup . . .

The melancholic who practise inamorato
The rites of rosary with sham devotion,
Reason that through such strategy
They will not be defrauded of Utopia
Should it happen to exist . . .

And yet through this envenomend curtain
Creeps a driblet of ameliorating Charity –
Aware of human foibles and only praying
Deliverance from the potential wickedness
Which they know well does dwell within . . .

Inconversant with all the divers heresies
Spoken in the name of God, and the labyrinth
Of theological ambiguity whose abstruse meaning
Sow seeds of doubt in otherwise contented minds,
There are a few who fill their days with
Good works and quiet meditation . . .

[*cont.*

They shun the ostentatious oratory of those
Who would by mass-communication convince
The innocent and gullible of their power
To grant a way to Heaven's gate, but lead
Their followers to nowhere but a barren land.

It is they, the good Samaritans,
Who daily bathe and tend the pendant sacrifice
Of the suffering Son of Man . . .

1970

Undercurrent

I can guess why writers rise at five and start again
To plumb the passages of their fertile minds
And clear their overburdened souls or seek to fix
The fleeting fancies of a lonely ego in the night,
Restless in some manner to assuage the horrors
Generated by the overwrought or sick imagination
Which strives to somehow quench the shock
Of a sudden revelation of the kind
That lights the darkness with a negative charge
And validates a version of perverted truth
That kills the will and renders everything in vain.

Avid for diversion to drown the jangled numbers
Of the circuit, that remind us to review
The manner of our way, and automatic hone our pace
In that enervating final furlong that we feeble-minded fear,
Yet despite fatigue sustain within our cooling core.
Deserted by a daunting, diminishing vitality
And the haunted hope and contemplation of a strange
Unconscious re-admittance to that dark and distant place
Where experience so painfully acquired is lost
And good fortune granted is annulled;
Where science and technology delude and finally betray us
With the Judas kiss of truth which teaches us to fear
The natural, the simple, and the empirically sound.

So that when our elements, transmogrified
In that mysterious cleansing vault
The day before the day that we were born -
Where the once beyond-redemption we,
All imperfection now dispersed, are re-introduced
Into this unique, perhaps fantastic world
Yielding our consciousness to yet another whimsical utopia
Free from sickness, warfare, accident, and natural disaster.

Enigma

And so this vagrant globe in every way
Spins through the ages, unable to repel
The gathering momentum of those forces good and ill
The occult wickedness and virtues of the mind
The twisting, warping influences of Life
Or the contentment and understanding of the spirit.

Like some ancient sailing ship braving the stormy seas,
Is Life – a monotonous rising and falling
From crest to trough with awful helpless certainty
The highest aspirations of Man combined and mixed
With his most bestial and miserable depths
All with the finality and certainty of Death.

Does this voyage fraught with so much danger and delight
Serve not to teach new generations moral hope
And respect for those who have already braved
These stormy seas of worldly good and evil?
And yet, have we no right to fight a million times
For freedom which is indeed our birthright?
Our seas are no less foreign and elements no less inclement
Than those of lesser men in lesser ages.

Is the increasing opportunity for the exploitation
Of everything, all that can justify our being?
Or does another shore beckon us?
An island of spectres, ancient mariners
Clamouring amid the din of damnation for a hearing
Only to be drowned among the jagged foamy rocks
Thundering the wrath of the supreme master "Fools!
They do not hear", and even if they could
They would heed you not!
Only the eyes of the dead are opened . . .

1970

Old Age

Distortion

Who's that in the mirror?
I really do not know
He kind of looks familiar
But his hair's like driven snow
His skin is old and wrinkled
It really can't be me
For I'm still young and vital –
As productive as can be.
It's true I can't remember
Phone numbers very well
Nor dates and years like sixty-three –
Or where I put my key
Where the North-West Frontier is
And who was Syngman Rhee.
What day it was your mum gave birth
So many years ago
What in age you would become
And how you'd further grow
For you've got talent, time and love
And of the three I'd rather have
The first, the second and the third
And who cares if I get the bird?
If I get hurt, it matters not
My short-term memory's all but shot
And happenings of recent days
Are more or less forgot.
So please forgive an old man's ways
All the *malentendus* and farces
As he reviews his final days
And tries to find his glasses . . .

2016

In Vino Veritas

What great big eyes you make Mama
When I get near the truth
In the presence of our grandsons
Who need to know forsooth
What goes on in the silence of an ageing mind
Where there are no sacred cows
Nor prejudicial thoughts of any kind.
For young lads have a right to know
The unadulterated facts of life
So that they will only good seeds sow
And do their best in later life . . .

Old Man's Lament

I know why old men smell of pee
Because they drink so much you see.
And drop their dinner down their shirts
When one time easy movement hurts.

I know why they get annoyed
With prejudices unalloyed.
These ancient bigots huff and puff
And cannot cope with modern stuff

Like tattooed, bolted, mutilated faces
And those who lack the social graces.
The male who wears his hat indoors
And all the joys of Faith deplores.

Football, competition, war,
Celebrities and what they're for –
Computers, rap and sporting fashion
They hate these things with greatest passion

They pity those who cannot hold a fork
And those who don't eat fish or pork.
Those who speak with loaded mouth
And care not if they seem uncouth.

Quick to complain and criticise
But slow impatience to disguise.
Their great knowledge they intone –
But not without a magic phone!

And what of those who use the planet's good
While damage done's not understood
They leave their litter on the ground
And fly tip rubbish where it won't be found.   [cont.

Old Age

Only spectators and followers of fame
They pontificate but never play a game.
Others cheat and lie their way through life
And when found out resort to bullet and the knife

Expressed in oft times stupid, racist cant
Against another view they rant.
Undisciplined, they let their tempers rise
And innocent opinion violently chastise.

Children of the social net and masters of the game
Whose knowledge of their native tongue is lame
Compared to foreigners – those seen as fools
Who speak so well because they learn the rules.

Old gentlemen forget important things
While memory passing sadness brings.
Infirm, they need stout sticks to walk
And fall asleep when tedious people talk.

The obese-cyclists who clog our ways
Whose unwise diets truncate their days,
Enslaved by substances they can't resist
And spectacle that can't be missed . . .

Sentiment, fake art and Kitsch seem fine,
Pretence and fraud to some are genuine.
Lack of judgement among the young and bold
Is to be expected, but not among the old.

Football scores and rituals of any kind
Are enough to glaze the sensors of our mind
And start our wretched snoring –
Especially when the conversation's boring.

When I no more can hold my water
And need a surgical supporter
I'll know why some old men smell of pee
'Cause one of them is surely me . . .   2015

Cul-de-Sac

Thou euphemistic bastion of senility
Called eventide by those of midday mien
Who contemplate thy function with detachment
As they their youthful independence wean
On fleeting pleasures of a present time,
Designed to shroud a short mortality
And obviate the readiness to meet
That canine spectre of fidelity
Pursuing those a natural span allowed
But partaking in Man's dogged coalition
Until with sudden undetected skill
It herds them through their torpid gates' demission.

Grim prisons of a million condemnèd cells
Surrounded by Victorian brick and apathy
Within earshot of those ancient preparation bells
Summoning in vain the dandering gypsy of Youth
And oblivious disciples of Diana blindly forward
Of saddened tongues' experience blithely unconcerned
And by the pit of Fate's dark and cowardly steward.

But what of those etiolated gargoyles who await
In isolated dotage the casketed release
And much-lauded reconciliation with pioneer souls
Who likewise longed before their own decease?
Who from within these gelid walls of uselessness
Suffer the slow garrotte of gendered isolation
For reasons of a clinical and unsympathetic state
Where love-letters of a second childhood transend
An institution to dissipate the loneliness and grief
Of wedded separation, and to maintain a little self-respect....

[cont.

142

The flower or the apple transported by pathetic means
To the unforgotten lover, once the innocently blushing
Recipient of those romantic rhymes of happier hours
Before that effete descent into melancholy.
And a bathotic state of atrophying agèdness!
Its knowledge of vitality so short!
Its agony of frustrated progress!
By that narrow torrent of heartbeats
Upon whose brink we try to keep our equilibrium
Until the autumn-tide allows another fragile leaf to fall
And drift forevermore upon the gentle breeze of time

No more sensations that benumb –
No more solutions to the code –
No more emollient dreams of Life to come,
For Life has reached its promised antipode . . .

1979

Old Age

Like some wretched fuel-deprivèd pauper
On a misty winter's evening gazes
Into the embers of life's slowly fading fire
And tries to stave off the everlasting chill
Of those final draughts of human frailty
Which whisper around with eerie invitation.

A disconcerting harlot of the shadows,
Luring on her prey with promises of elysian delight
Only rendered unattractive by the price –
The bankrupting levy of final unconsciousness,
But nevertheless on occasions sought
By those so rich in worldly completion or despair
That they desire a premature effacement.

Half-afraid to stir those dying coals
Lest in concentrated effort they
Collapse and die before their time.
Unable to heap on any nuggets of reprieve,
But loath to quit the feebly flickering rest
Of that consuming blaze which still stirs
With clarity in the youthful chasms of memory –

– That ill-begotten dweller in the past
Recalling with regret its infantile potential
Squandered by its later lack of luck,
Or contemplating sadly impotence and age
With its vast treasure trove of hope
But not able to bequeath such wealth
To brash unwilling heirs.

[*cont.*

Old Age

Drawing close the flimsy shawl of comfort
Around resigned and stooping shoulders,
While ornate hands transmogrify
Their idle sweep and steady tick
Into the whirring blur of bloody blade
About to be the agent of release
Of an emasculated prisoner, cruelly confined.

For the faithful, heaven's promise
Too often relied on for their spiritual good,
And for the infidel a frantic reckoning up
Of dogma, liturgy, and sin (or none of these)
But for both, a time of preparation to depart
An era with no personal remembered start nor end –
Only the duration and quality of its interim . . .

1980

Mirror

Bland speculum of falsity
Deluding those who come to gaze
With satisfaction or reproof
On shallow, petty human ways!

No crack of imperfection thine
No indiscretion stains thy charm
No ripple sinister disturbs
Thy innocent lacustrine calm.

Defenceless as a child you hang
Suspended by the nail of time
Upon a wall of inane space
Condemned unto a life of mime.

Like some great ashen cliff of kelp
Which dumbly echoes fleeting light
In isometric waves of sham
Beyond the paltry range of sight.

Reflected marquetry of Man
Veneered with sundry attribute
Thy crystalline morality
Reveals its crust of earthy lute!

Beneath a glaze of charity
To those of introspective mien
Who contemplate with bitterness
The foetus of what might have been.

[*cont.*

Old Age

Refracted by its own free will
It petrifies between the gloom
Of monstrous truth too dark to see
And fabricated value's tomb.

But those happy martyred souls
Who view with passion, silvered face
Rebounded flaw and deadly sin
And shadows of a better place,

Await their turn to step behind
That tantalizing limbo plate
Away from all that would conceal
A vision of their mirrored fate.

But deprecate not silent one
Each sanctimonious pseudonym
Which ricochets with deadly aim
According to Creation's whim

From off thy misused countenance –
Ground to reflect and not to damn,
To witness in perplexity
And sadly mimic mortal man.

Pattern for Defeat

Heredity

Who can with superficial understanding
Speculate on matters of a hidden past
And judge a host of tangled circumstance
With preconception's likewise addled logic?

For all the factors of enduring human type
Which lurk in ever-changing combination
Within the treasure caves of generation
Evade the very essence of conjecture.

But they regardless of condition wait
With ill-concealèd restlessness
A passionate release and subsequential blending
In the secret workshops of the womb.

It is a living legacy of mystic art
Which blankly bears the latent imperfections
And undreamed qualities of Nature.

It is substance born of common stock
And coaxed to new virginity
By evolution's unaccounted course.

Crude pulp emerges thus as parchment
To wait the pattern of the scribe,
Who with perverse or bless'd intent
Will utilize its infinite potential
According to the dictates of his will.

Environment

But wills are subject to a living state
And what we in an egocentric transcience
With fretful satisfaction dub experience,
Is little but a chaos of traditionalism
And the related rituals of routine.

Yet this condition of inherited confusion
Is condoned, nay lauded by those
Afforded not the sacrifice of thought
As they like empty sponges suck
The venom of prefabricated sentiment.

They choose not to view the mind
As a device of delicate construction
Which programmed by an unseen hand
Must take all stimuli unto itself,
But rather as some secret catacomb
Filled with vaguely occult echoes.

Compelled to work without discrimination,
It transcribes the mass that moves the mass
And as a random consequence creates
The contradicting character of Man –
Characteristics of a life which swarms
With misconceptions and unlikely gems as numerous
As the micro-organisms which crawl
Upon some slightly tainted fruit.

Conformity

Absorbing all the doctrines of the plot
We vegetate in dusty rows of bigotry
And find the unearned comfort sought
In warm but stunted infecundity.

Thus in the breeze of changing mood
We cling with withered haunted roots
To soil of long denuded trust,
Clutching our seed to selfish bloom
Lest they should waft away
From the protection of our sacred rule
To lodge in loamy meadows
Of contrasting but progressive wit.

Allegorical gardens threaten punishment
Or exile from an order rebelliously defied.
A bogus acquiescence is less painful
Than the ridicule of those
Who have succumbed and can no longer bear
Their youthful retrospective dreams.

For them decisions of a personal morality
Still sting like gaping wounds
Whose only analgesic is a bleak conformity
Or collusion – a return to that most secret place
Where they take all their nourishment
From the cord of Nature's ancient order
Which conceived and bore them
To the exclusion of everything else
Which might precipitate a painful spewing out
Into a world without the comfort of support . . .

1980

Comfort

This damned self-preservation
With all its lies and implication!
What sort of hateful breed are we who emulate
The bloody traits of ancestors long-lost
Who trod their hypocritic ways
Before the advent of recorded time?
Seeking the instinctive opiates
Of power and sexual saturation,
We arrest undreamed-of psychic powers
And stay the sordid beasts we are –
But docile ones it seems as we
With apprehensive conscience rush
In the diurnal dilemma of duty
To profitable tasks which earn us
The security we crave in return
For our unquestioned subservience.
Taught our tricks like performing seals
To do the bidding of the masters
Of our larders – capitalists or visionaries
Who try in turn to buy their own assurance.
Through the pitch of their imaginary moment
We are swept along in tidal waves
Of marketing deception while they succeed,
With all the mighty means they have to hand,
In bonding the belief of their unwitting slaves
That their provincial pettiness has worth.

Policy

Vile politics seducer of the simple!
This governmental rule-book of control
Which robs and beats initiative
And punishes with pious wig and gown
The indiscretions of an immature opinion.

But dictums are for parlour games
And order is evolved through simple honest trial –
Not the mumbo-jumbo of expedience
Nor ignorance's easily persuaded mirth.

Are we naïve enough to view the maxims
Of pragmatic law without suspicion,
Or say that we possess our thoughts
When mass control is so insidious?

A subtle drug released by the few
Who wield the plume of economic envy
When there is profit to be made
Through simple bending of the sense of words.

Yet he who can escape the sticky web
Of propaganda's dreadful toxic truths
Which interchange the strength of growth and right
And wash away all natural defences of the brain,

Scorned, derided – held in such contempt
By the arachnoid smugness of the trade –
Rich shareholders of the poverty of others
And investors in the rampant misery of debt.

Doctrine

How eagerly we suck the bitter potions
Prescribed by those conceited quacks
Who strut the parquet-flooring of our times
And charge the dreadful bleeding fees
That honest men cannot afford to pay!

Their patients are the crippled ones
Who cannot walk without a crutch
Or those whose bogus blindness hides
The symptoms of far greater ill.

The deaf who can but hear the voices
Of cheap ambition's social gain
And likewise those who for some therapeutic purpose
Mouth the magic recipes of peace

In imitation of a stronger will,
And in their humbled ignorance consult
The vaunting certainties of Man.

Indolence comes here to pass the day
With false complaints invented off the cuff
To cheat his master of his hire
And to evade the higher labour of reflection.

But all resume their various roles content
In their acceptance of the humbug
Which provides the table of the charlatan
Gladly they remit complicity's exacting price
For such is the convention of the times . . .

Apathy

What dreamer does not wish for change
Or hope with optimism's bold escape
That ills of unsung centuries will fade
As dusk gives way to certain light
Without the paltry effort of misguided hands?

He tarries but a lifetime with his folly
And wakes but once to heed the knell of truth
Which summons him to final sleep.
He sees that his self-centred toil
Has elevated not the smallest undulation
Upon the unplumbed seas of human destiny.

This is pessimism's most triumphant phase –
A natural despair soon after neutralised
By the declining faculties of age
When the intolerable risks of Youth
Deprive the jaws of death their teeth.

But even this façade of perspicacity
Dissolves along the margins of our reason,
Here teachings of the finite world

Overlap and contradict each other
Til freedom is a crushing last
And bondage is the clue to ecstasy.

Thus out of the convulsions of defeat,
Great ponderous stones are poured and set
To grind the husks of insignificance.

Mutation

Locked within the vault of empty speculation
Among the half-truths of our own creation,
We languish on imprisoned by the basic senses,
Suffering those born not less imperfect
Than ourselves to grope a darkened mortal stage
In rôles of preachers, demi-gods and judges.
These are the frustrated fabricants of truth
Who use the cunning subterfuge of rank
In their coercion of an aimless innocence.
But even midst the throes of this condition
There stands a type of man alone
Who with a quiet voice of self-respect,
Demands a hearing in the name
Of Goodman's long-disregarded cause,
And those who seek the salve of hope
Would do exceeding well to give them ear
He is not the vendor of dry platitudes
Which barely stirred the sleeping pews of yore,
Nor is he Dogma's loud but ageing pawn,
For he has splendour of his own.
Like he who went before him as a teacher
Of new value who presses not his meaning
On unworthiness but sorrows for the babble
Of righteousness's loose befuddled tongue,
Which brings us to a lingering restlessness
Or the privations of unspeakable bondage.

The Wall

How we with pious brows deplore
The hasty structures of opposing thought,
Raised to protect the feeble mind within
Whose unaccepted failure rules unchecked
The personal fortunes of a simple people
Held in the bondage of political insulation
By the gabions of its own mistrust.

How we in indignation curse
The cold rough surface of misunderstanding's block
Held rigid in the ever-hard'ning grasp
Of reinforced suspicion's mortar'd hand.
But the eye of higher discernment is frustrated
By blinding baffles and the sensitive ear
Is filled with amplified stupidity.

How we despise the guardians of that wall
As they their uniform delinquence flaunt
With the threatening arms of destructive inhibition
Beyond the grasp or experience of an intellect
Stunted by the narcotic of a propaganda
Which echos round bizarre enforcements
Of a grey and crumbling delusion.

How we with horror contemplate
The inmates of expediency's cruel prison
Divorced from marriage with reality
By the master-mason's sand and lime,
Erected to harbour a bogus sentiment
Or shield the damaged psyche
From the sceptical waves of alleged normality.

[*cont.*

How we with pity murmur prayers
For souls that languish in a tomb
Of living death and dying hope,
And laud psychotic tunnels of escape
Of those who beg asylum's peace
According to the personal assimilation
Of a concrete but one-sided obstruction.

God preserve the Man
From the inaccuracies of rumour
And the relativity of circumstance!
He has always found the scapegoat
For his own inadequacies
Through intolerance – so builds he walls
To hide his insecurity.

Heidelberg 1963
In memory of the erection of the Berlin Wall 1962 and its
removal in 1989. (Both witnessed on ARD)

Door

A door of mystery resounding with the knocks
Of those impatient to control the lives of others
And yet an awesome block from whence
Those who have already found the key
Mete out their judgements upon lesser men.

Patiently, we sit on benches of our own ambition
Prey to the contempt and ruthlessness of stronger men.
In cold corridors of power we anxiously await
Acceptance into the sphere of power and influence.

The sounds of battle echo from within
And even from such lowly aspect
We may witness all the pitfalls of incumbency
While we endure the body cramps of conscience.

On, on we wait, for who are we not to accept
The stereotyped philosophy of those
Who dwell in comfort and security at the expense
Of puppets which they with such dexterity manipulate?

Behind that oaken portal of respectability
Noble birth, luck and honeyed talk the masters
Of our future legislate our lives
While we await their condescending call.

Why do we remain here with the sweating palms
And aching buttocks of our discontent?
Have we no home or are we spiritually
Incapable of walking the boards alone?

[*cont.*

Old age waits here in stupefaction or despair
Dying for an invitation to the board within
And in the end succumbing to a final failure
Of having played one's part in someone else's game.

Some of us have waited far too long already
In this unfriendly place where status rules the roost,
We are but helpless, trusting chickens
Doomed to feed the egos of a wealthy caste . . .

Personalities

Highlands Queen

Gladys's birthday's come again
So many times since way back when
It was not only rude; it was an outrage
To dwell upon a lady's age.
But her good friends here today
Their Highlands Queen to tribute pay
And mark this saintly woman's birth
With memories, drinks and mirth
Thanks to Louise who lends a venue cool
Fork supper, friends and music, as a rule
Don't count the numbers; contemplate
We only came to celebrate
A gentle, generous lady, full of fun
Who cheers the lives of everyone!

Putz Fairy

She is the one without conceit
Who cleans my house
And keeps my laundry neat.
She makes me foods
That I can freeze
She sympathises
When I'm on my knees
And when my crumbling back's a strain
She quickly banishes the pain
With strong hands
And German stuff
Until I've really had enough.
She on occasions checks my feet
But keeps her services discreet
And when at last
She has to go
It's true to say
I miss her so . . .

Tribute to Steve Cutts (Animator)

Mindlessly we all consume
The bounty of the Earth
Because we know its price
But often not its worth
In terms of money which we need
The children of our souls to feed
And then the lust for other things
The rape of Nature brings
'Til we, not disconcerted
While all of worth is being converted
To items which cannot be bought
And which in schools were seldom taught
Our air, our water, a healthy way of life
A planet free of hate and strife
Of ignorance, superstition and the like
Ill health, catastrophe and death . . .
We sometimes justify the wrong
And demonise the right with tricks
To prove how clever are our politics
When unity was strength and Presidents were wise
The World seemed safer, a place to ponder
And at the mystery of its origin to wonder
But we still heal luxury pursue
While others far less fortunate than we
Find only starvation, disease and cold
To comfort them as they grow old
Victims of having been born in a dangerous time and place
And even of belonging to onother colour, faith or race
And not conforming to the thoughts purveyed
On some tweeting, blogging, bragging page
Of malcontents and the unfulfilled consumed with rage.

The Investigator

Persistence was my brother
Once called Nanki Poo
A daring little boy-babe
Who looked a bit like you
He never did what he was told
He would not be confined
Within his room or in his cot
From whence he often climbed,
And filled us all with dread.
He each year grew more bold until,
One day escaping from his bed
He injured something (so we thought)
Which turned his waters red.
Panic got his mother on her feet
To seek a doctor right away
But the only thing that they found out
On that most frightening day
Was that the greedy little brat
Had eaten lots of baby beet!
High gates, roofs, ladders, furniture
Were all a challenge to this curious boy
Who when he didn't break his neck
His need to win transformed to joy.

[*cont.*

A stubborn, disobedient child
Causing tears, fears and despair
To parents, teachers and the rest
Until relieved they saw him go,
To England, join the Met, by heck
Become the keenest bobby yet.
Where due to his tenacious bent
He soon became a first-class 'tec
With his mate Martin always on the hop
Taking risks and difficult to stop.
He loved the work arresting crooks
And as for rules, he threw away the books
And later left the country – plan in mind
In pastures new, new challenges to find.
Leaving London problems behind him far,
And that he did with Carlos and the Car
And the British Army of the Rhine
Where he played many parts,
Breaking more than several hearts
And while avoiding serious sin
Made lots of dosh in Old Berlin
And in an ancient Saxon land
Reverted to his former skills
Analysing fraud and strife,
Pursuing the wicked out of hand
Before returning to his eyrie
With no sign of being weary . . .

2017

Under the Bushel

When will you
Make me wise
And tell me who resides
Behind those
Non-communicative eyes
. . . of yours?
What do you have
To hide from me?
Who only needs
To hear a breath of truth
Which tells me
Your concerns and all
The disappointments
And the bad decisions
You refuse to share
Or let unguarded slip,
Nor even jesting mention
When you're in your cups . . .
Ho bisogno d'un
Fratello simplice'
Comme il faut, mais pas
Quelqu'un qui se cache
Derrière la figure.
D'un autre . . .
Qui n'ose d'exprimer
Les verités de sa vie,
Ses peurs et ses esperances
Pour l'avenir . . .

[cont.

Un frère sans maskes
Sans secrets et qui
Raconte avec joies
Et regrets les histoires
De sa vie et de ses amours.
Un homme avec qui
Je partage le sentiment
Que nous nous n'avons
Peu de chose en commun . . .

2018

Mons Meg[*]

The captain's on his quarter deck
And the Canons Pound away
I can hear them down below
Where you wisely warned me
I would go,
If I didn't mend my ways,
And on the saintly Clement days
Be a little more like you,

Attending to the garden
Pruning all your roses
Tearing down the vine
We hope these healthful actions
Make you feel divine . . .
Thinking up new sermons
For better or for ill
Before you finish roaming
And vanish o'er the hill.

Past achievements fleeting fall
But you continue to walk tall
In spite of age you're sharp of mind,
Your gait still seen along the wynd
Playing your part in our old parish
With good-humour – not unkind
A comfort to the Welsh and Scottish
And surely in St Peter's tome recorded
A long, illustrious life to be rewarded.

2016

---

[*] A mighty medieval cannon at Edinburgh Castle

Napier's Last

Free at last from pain and stress
Souter Jonnie's gone away
And left us sad and Sandy.
Now cobbling in the Milky Way
A glass of vodka near at hand
He's teaching the starlets how to swear,
And be, like him, a one-man band.

He often waxing lyrical would recall
Drunken pop stars and their hits
Obliging girls who gave their all
Tackety boots, the old Glaswegian wits
Like Nesbit, Connolly and McCall.
Barrowland, the "washie", Crossmyloof
The Clyde, Birthplace of a thousand ships.

We mourne his life in retrospect
Exponent of the leather trade
He knew how to cut and stretch and buff it
To grip and nip and punch and scuff it
He fobbed us off with keyrings, trees and creams
Fixed stilettos, accessoires beyond our dreams
And showed us how to skive.

While cutting keys, repairing shoes and selling locks
He entertained us in his kingdom every week
With tales of football, and other famous jocks.
Wherever there's a worn-out sole
And heels with motives rotten
John the Cobbler, Blessèd Scotsman of this Parish

Will never, ever be forgotten!

2018

Ale Warning

O Billy, Billy
Where are you?
We hope you haven't
Got the 'flu
We miss you frightfully
You see
But you'll be working
On a client's PC.
Come back to us
When you are free
So fuck the work
On yon PC
For with us girls
You'll happy be.
We'll have some drinks
And eat some links[†]
With egg and chips to boot
And then we'll a' gae
Doon the toon
An hae oorsels
A rare auld stooshy
At the hoose of
Jock Muldoon . . .

2016

[†]   Sausages

Fantasy Girl

You are the girl whom
I have met too late
As I with apprehension
My effacement wait.

You are the girl
That I might get
By chance, but tardily
And with a measure of regret.

You are the girl
Capricious chance
Has introduced to me
My passing to enhance.

You are the girl
Who fills my ageing heart
With dread
For soon I must depart.

You are the girl
Who complacency destroys
For I am old
And can't compete with other boys.

You are the girl
I did not expect to meet
In this familiar place
From whence there's no retreat

You are the girl
Lurking in the shade
Of a contented, stable life
Some say by God's own blacksmith made.

[*cont.*

You are the girl
Who could destroy
The peaceful nature of my muse
Transmogrifying grief to sinful joy.

You are the girl
Whose spontaneity, sympathy and wit
Convert my thoughts to love
As mental miracles befit.

You are the girl
Whom I in vain attended
Throughout my virgin years
Until my youth was mended.

You are the girl
Enhancing all my dreams
But drifting sadly from my life
And all its mystical regimes.

You are the girl
I nightly longed to hold
When I was young
But not uncouthly bold.

You are the girl
Who comes to me in sleep
Enhancing all the dreams
That I would wish to keep.

You are the girl
Who tells me things that might have been
Had I been born in other times
And in a more exotic scene.

You are the girl
With many years to live
In happiness and sadness
And comfort to another free to give.

[cont.

You are the girl
Who fills my days with peacefulness and light
(My spirit glad to be alive)
My nights with sensual delight.

You are the girl
With many years to live
And comfort to some
Undeserving soul to give.

You are the girl
Sweet irony of Fate!
Who In spite of my devotion
Does not seek an agèd mate.

You are the girl
Who was tailor-made for me
Who seemed the answer to my prayers
And yet was not to be.

You are the girl
Who makes me glad however
But also sad that our two paths
One day will sadly part forever.

2017

Harold – Parting Friend

Goodbye to one we grew to love
Of ancient race and differing creed,
Who by chance crossed o'er our way
And richness in our pattern wove
With many a thoughtful word and deed.

Au revoir to friendship true,
Short as the shutter's urgent action,
Exposing life's dull plate of woe
To the brilliant light of few
Who pierce the filter of selection.

Aufwiedersehen to gentleness,
Dedicated to the art
Of tending those laid low upon
The bed of physical distress
With learning and the healing dart.

Farewell to his integrity
With unaffected view of Life,
That quiet absence of conceit
And hidden sensitivity
Laid bare by warm affection's knife.

May his love of classic beauty
Sustain his spirit through each season,
May his God afford him comfort
In times of what seems hopeless duty
And guide the dictates of his reason.

Bon voyage to one admired
As he sets out for pastures new,
May health and wisdom shadow him
In all achieved or just aspired.
To a parting friend – Adieu!   1963

Taking the Mickey

A northern spirit wedded to his Jan
The temple's fragrant smoker (cencer)
And a man who does not erect barriers (fencer)
Member of a highly intellectual class (Mensa)
He knows what he needs to get ahead
Lover of the sartorial elegance
He does not care for dirty, beastly hairy dogs or cats
Because he has a special feeling for unusual hats
He dispels my vapours with good red wine (condenser)
And hospitality wonderfully fine
Not brutish – a gentleman is he
He does not flex his tensing muscles (tensor)
On any rough boy's sport, you see
But gladly with his friends holds court
Providing drinks and lots of fun (dispenser)

Aly Baby

Nicol has a blonde bird
She comes in every day
She makes his bed
She tends his feet
And sees that he is fed.

She rises early every day
And comes on foot from Ore
She buys him milk
She brings him jam
And provisions of that ilk.

She makes him take his pills, you know
She cleans the house as well
She does the wash
She irons shirts
She helps the lonely, poor or posh.

She's never heard to loud complain
A cheerful girl is she
Much loved by all
She plays the game
Among us she walks tall . . .

Musings on a precious cleaner.

Relationships

Anniversary

It is the memory of a joyful occasion when,
Despite misgivings, one takes a step into
The darkness of a future quite unknown
With a like-spirit that one unlikely found
And slowly learned to love and trust,
But whom you may never fully understand.
Little does one contemplate the consequences
Of what may spring from the content of this,
This extraordinary union, blessèd or condemned
But it will bear the hallmarks of the caring nature
Of your character, education and experience.
The gentle caring for each other's needs
Must not be forgotten nor ever taken for granted
For it is the loyalty and unstinted devotion,
The capacity to forgive and forget our frailties
The keeping of one's counsel and the peace
That forms the unplanned but stable platform
For the generation to come, yet we little thought
That it would be in the unexpected shape of
A brilliant Artist and astute, prolific Author
And a first-class Lawyer and amazing Sinologue.
Despite our many differences, our concord seems
To have weathered most of the storms of life
And does not deserve the rich rewards of knowing
Two fine, sincere young men, diligent and kind
With whom we proudly entrust our hopes and aspirations
For the future of our antique but still surviving Love . . .

2016

Erinnerungen

Your heart is in Celle
Your heart is not here
Your heart is in Celle
With all you hold dear
With Thomas and Corinna –
The loving way these two
Your evening meal they fix
Alcoholic, creamy, rich.
In the Postmeister's fine old cellars
Where you meet those lovely fellers
You have known and loved for years.
Horst and Moni, Len' and Toddy
Irene, Christine of the lovely body,
China Kallé, Rolf and Fredericke
Jean Priol of Bockelskamp and Silke.
How can you live without them – how?
While meaning much to you, I vow
Are they present in your dreams
And memories of your high-up place
Above this old romantic space?
Strolling the Aller river down
Across Pfennigbrücke, into town
Down the Stechbahn, walking tall
Through the woodlands in the fall –
Saxon culture and your 'family' kiss
These, I'm sure are what you'll miss.

2016

Forget Not Thy Brother

Forget not thy brother, urgent squire
As thou with selfish motivations steal
Like ever-lengthening twilight shadows
Across the no-man's land of mortal time.
In trepidation waiteth he the overwhelming tide
Of human lust and selfishness, which o'er him would ride.

Ignore not thy brother, urgent squire
Lest he in panic, thinking you a fiend
Doth by foul means contrive to hasten
For reason primitive, your partial end.
No friendly call to trust, his ill-timed vacillation heeds
For hope to live must bear the barbs of Jason's spiky seeds.

Doubt not thy brother, urgent squire
As thou with all the caution of the Wild
By many a devious route approach
The undetermined factor of his wit.
Impeded by the rotting stumps of trees of Earthly pride,
That choked by creepers of mistrust, achieving nothing died.

Betray not thy brother, urgent squire
As thou his daunted visage dost survey –
A mask of stark uncertainty.
Salute this creature with your trembling hand,
For cruel political expediency lies here with gloomy dread,
Mated with suspicion's whore – conveniently wed.

Leave not thy brother, urgent squire
When he in joy accepts your friendship's blood
With moistened eyes of wonderment
At Man's unmanly attribute fulfilled.
For actions of unselfish love extend thy global lease,
So with like courage bear thy sons and go thy way in peace.

Thinking of You Again

To those I have neglected
But always much respected
I send my heartfelt greeting
For since our last delightful meeting
My ageing faculties continually fail,
And what is left of me grows frail
I feel a warm and loving bond
When I recall our friendship fond.
As every wanton year slips by
Reminding me that all must die;
That in the scheme of things
To be conscious sadness brings
For there is a price exacted
By every whit of joy extracted,
During this small window
Which the gods of Nature us endow.
Though robbed of energy and will
I delight in memories of you still.
More problematic to sustain
Are thoughts of future life arcane
For as my mind and memory decline
Consciousness becomes a strangely altered thing;
Perceptions lacking truth like tempting sirens sing
No longer strong in times inclement
Still defiant, but not so independent
I cling to those who help me cope,
And thanks to you, retain some hope.

2019

Songs and Anthems

Second Chance

(So) I am coming home to you [beloved]
(For) I have been away too long.
We parted long ago
For reasons of a hasty hand,
That now I cannot understand.
For I still love you as I did then. # (refrain?)

There seems to be no more a reason
For us to be so far apart
While we so yearn to be as one, [my sweet]
Lying together – a magic time –
When I was yours and you were mine
I love you now as I did then. #

So we should try it all again
Now that we are more mature
Despite our diff'ring natures, [precious girl]
You pleased me in so many ways –
Upon your skin my loving gaze.
For we shall love again as we did then. #

So I am coming home to you this time
An older and a wiser man
For I have made mistakes, [my dear]
Regretting all these wasted years –
My disregard of all your fears.
This time we'll love better than we did then. #

2016

Provisional Words for the music to "The Road Back Home"
  (Polo Piatti)

England

Mother of democracy
Fortress of the sea
Refuge for the sorely pressed
Longing to be free.

Verdant valleys in the spring
Budding beauty in the field!
And on the margins of the way
Wildlife wand'ring in the weald.

In secret places of the mind
I see your rivers, lakes and streams.
Dales and dells and ghylls in spate
Delight my soul and fill my dreams.

Ancient ruins long undone,
Manor houses built to last
Saxon barns and watermills,
Farms and forges from the past.

Stately homes down winding lanes
The glory of a new-mown lawn,
Patient cattle at the gate
Waiting for the coming dawn.

Songbirds, insects, butterflies
In the warming healing sun
The heady scent of blossoms sweet
When tardy summer has begun.

[cont.

Sultry flowery countryside
Pollen-laden worker bees
Ewes and lambs on meadows green
And hungry nestlings in the trees.

Rocky shores and sandy bays
Exciting sometimes-hidden caves
Antique fishing boats and nets
Crabby pools and foam-flecked wave.

Medieval castles
Parks and Tudor Halls
Charming tiny hamlets
Whose history enthralls.

Timeless tides and seasons
Memories of the sea
England regal England
You are home to me!.

2010

Appendix
Symbolic Meditations

Originally published in
Bruce Nicol (2016) *Cryptograph*

Artifact

Victim of our
own innocence
we seek order
and a meaning
to our mental
flood through
the symbolism
of the moment
Catch-words and rousing prayers, peddled by pithy
priests and politicians stimulate a mass of false
emotion and empty sentiment in the reflex regions
of the mind and construct cages for prefabricated
passion – not for the general wellbeing of Mankind
but merely to control the actions of the ignorant
Thus we allow
our powers of
higher reason
to steal away
into a gloomy
state of mind
where bigotry
blinds vision
and causes us
to steal away
to a pleasant
incarceration
where a corps
of automatons
caring naught
for the needy
and oblivious
of their lack
as insolently
they defend a
doctrine they
do not desire
to understand

Democracy

Democracy is like
the corpse which in
its degradation leads
the false life of decay
& breeds within a bastard
cell of promise passed away.
Thus rigor's truth below doth
lie beneath the soiled and deep
design which Nature's habit hides
and fetid life from vital death
eternally divides. That maudlin
hand which gravely tends with
longings for a spring unwound
and memory's shedding bloom
contrives sweet visions and
forgets corruption in the
tomb. Yet shrouded thinly
by the web of senseless
tongue and mindless eye
opposing forces reign
and rampant undermine
the flesh of Form's
exposed domain. Who
dares contemplate
a womb where free
corrosion gnaws
the gut seeking
the brass and
earth til all
those knots
of vitality
unwrought,
exact the
levy of
rebirth

1980

ID

In solitude
I probe the mind of man
For its conception of sense
Only to discover a sterile vacuum
Of traditional thought and prejudice.
I am alone in my travail but isolated not
From other men. I soliloquise but to fulfil
Profound longing for personal contribution to a
Forgotten cause of human awareness, understanding
And toleration of the philosophies which oppose the
Standards of my own hereditary limitations, yet other
Hearts shall echo all the murmurings of my conscience.
Insular by choice I try to gauge the depth of a shadowy
Potential already lost to those who have been robbed of
Faith by long exposure to Life's most tragic privations.
Anxieties of morbid logic in an atmosphere of comfortless
Egotism. Apart from other men am I, but conscious of that
Hopelessness which dogs their faltering steps. Distant am
I, but not insensitive to the rigour of aimlessness for
I am not entirely separated from my fellows. This would
Be to deprive myself of birthright for he is a fool or
Prophet who claims complicity with the Gods and I am
Neither. Therefore, I am indulgent towards those that
Call me brother, for who can alleviate the tensions
Of original thought when novelty is so surrounded
With uncertainty? Perception is a lonely island
Amid a heaving ocean of catastrophe, and he
Who sets sail into such tumult to comfort
The marooned soul is a friend indeed.
It is he who brings me the mantle
Of peace when I am consumed
With restlessness - for
I am a poet

Island

You lap around
My ragged shore
And penetrate the secret caverns of my being.
Your tides caress or lash my flanks
Depending on your unpredicted mood
But none can rob me of the comfort of thy mantel,
For even when the dismal winter mists
Obscure thy presence,
I can feel your bosom swell and
Hear the whisper of your tidings.
On clear days you can show me calm horizons
Far beyond the thunder of thy surf,
But at your height I am yet taller
For it is in my nature to be so.
No beacon stands upon my sod
To scatter droplets of illumination
Upon thy pregnant waters.
We hazard thus all those who would
Unbidden broach our restless congruence.
Where I am hard you smooth away
The jagged edge where other elements
Have split and scaled away my former self
And when a shattered part of me succumbs
And falls beneath your friendly flood,
It lies in peace until when you are low
You reach my loins and mingle with
Those stiller waters,
But always born of
Thee.

Rohrschach

What is it
it that evades
the mind yet leads
the spirit onwards in
that restless search for
Truth ? An elusive phantom
Is that which silently flits
Then margin of a mundane logic
And affords the straining inner
optic misty glimpses of Eternity
This is what inspires the visions
Of the poet and drives compulsive
fingers in their ceaseless craving
for perfection. It is the trump of
pragmatists, who, in their lust for
self-importance, beguile the simple
with hollow speculation. It is the
strength of those with faith enough
To give it name, but a vile scourge
to those imprisoned in the vault of
petty tangibility. It is the torch
that fires the matured imagination
and lifts the thinker to the very
portals of understanding yet bars
his access to absolute knowledge
With the limitations of his own
reason. It is a powerful hand
which grasps the counterpart
Of a wandering goodwill to
guide it to the paths of
higher motivation. It
is a certain force
that keeps its
mystery

Structure

Cells and
blocks to
confine a
wild will
within us

Categories concepts
And classes cloud a
Vision of universal
Harmony and balance
Inspiring obsessive
Little quests which
Stunt the intellect
Dendering delusions
Meritorious and all
Attainment rational

Structures are our passionate pretence
Our primitive possessions the a priori
Posture in which we cling concerned to
That which gave us birth or that which
We ourselves have sired. Restlessly we
Pace the shell of our incomprehensible
Inheritance. Embarrassed we survey the
Wind-swept dimensions of our ancestral
Preconception. Astonished we gaze upon
Its fragile fabrication and wonder how
It has endured so long. With an eye to
Profit we purge ourselves of prejudice
And plan comfortable compromises which
Will retain hereditary advantage. With
New mental blocks we subdivide the old
Transforming the familiar into novelty
Until absurdly gratified by the result
We rest a while within substantial but
Mutilated mansions of a malleable mind

1980

Confrontation

```
            Tempted by their
            Weakness fearful
            Of our imagining
            We witless weave
            A warlike way to
            win. Consumed by
            ancient fires we
            heed not warning
            nor the changing
            clock for strife
is born beyond the margin of the mind. Feigning
outrage we conscript the dreaming blood and call
the allied arsenal to arms until our focused fear
becomes the spearhead of a righteous confrontation +
Wearily we direct our secret forces at that field
Where only threat is foe and wrought-up delusion
Acts the unabating ally, where shots provide no
                    Immunity against
                    the weals of war
                    In vain shall we
                    Rejoice the seal
                    Of petty victory
                    For we must flex
                    the foil forever
                    Threats are thus
                    the precondition
                    for our survival
```

Confrontation

Tempted by their
weakness fearful
of our imagining
We witless weave
A warlike way to
win. Consumed by
ancient fires we
heed not warning
nor the changing
clock for strife
is born beyond the margin of the mind. Feigning
outrage we conscript the dreaming blood and call
the allied arsenal to arms until our focused fear
becomes the spearhead of a righteous **confrontation** +
wearily we direct our secret forces at that field
where only threat is foe and wrought-up delusion
Acts the unabating ally, where shots provide no
Immunity against
the weals of war
In vain shall we
Rejoice the seal
of petty victory
For we must flex
the foil forever
Threats are thus
the precondition
for our survival